Eating
without
Heating

**Favorite Recipes from Teens
Who Love Raw Food**

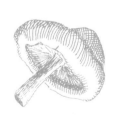

Sergei and Valya Boutenko
with illustrations by Valya Boutenko

Natural Zing
www.naturalzing.com
info@naturalzing.com

Raw Family Publishing

Distributed by:
www.Raw-food.com
POB 900202, SD, CA 92190
800-205-2350

Raw Family Publishing
2253 Highway 99 North, #58
Ashland, OR 97520

www.rawfamily.com

Photography on the front cover by Dragomir Vukovic

Edited by Shanti Einolander

Cover and interior design by Lightbourne

Library of Congress Control Number: 2002094433
ISBN 0-9704819-7-7

Disclaimer: Although Sergei and Valya Boutenko do not recommend cooked foods or standard medical practices, the information contained in this book is not intended as medical advice. The authors, publishers, and/or distributors will not assume responsibility for any adverse consequences resulting from adopting the lifestyle described herein.

*To our mom and dad for helping us
discover the joy of raw food.*

Contents

Notes From Sergei and Valya

Sergei:

Dear Children, Adolescents, and Adults,

I wish there were some way that I could get this message out to every single one of you. A message that would touch your lives and have you see that happiness is not sold in little baggies or a 40 oz. glass bottle. I wish that there were some way to show you, my own generation, that we can all be happy and free without drugs. I wish I could stop you from hurting your body and make you see how much you will regret it later in life.

Most of all, I wish that I could unite all of you and show you that every single one of you is beautiful and miraculous and that life would not be the same without you. Unfortunately, that is impossible, because the only way of teaching is actually not teaching at all! The only way I can get others to follow is by being a good example and sharing my story when asked. The words of even the wisest man are worth nothing if no one wants to hear them!

This is my story:

Before I ate raw food, I always wanted to be cool. I wore baggy pants with trendy names and had flashy skateboards and other toys, but for some reason I wasn't cool. The harder I tried, the less cool I was. When I started eating raw food, I hid it from my peers because I thought I would be even more un-cool. Later on, however, I found out that in their eyes eating raw food actually made me pretty cool. In fact, I noticed that a person doesn't even have to be way different to be cool. All one needs in order to be cool is sincerity.

Eating healthier made me more open. I stopped caring what people said and thought about me. I became more sincere and started speaking openly. People started noticing my sincerity and, as a result, I made new friends. When we are sincere, people gravitate toward us.

Are you or your children worried that by eating raw food you'll lose some friends? You might lose some friends, but I promise you, you'll gain three times as many quality new friends. If you are a raw fooder, it is best if you don't seclude yourself from the rest of the world and only hang out with raw fooders. You don't have to try to convert everybody to your "raw-ligion." In fact, it would be un-cool for you to say, "Stop eating that crap. That pizza's going to kill you." If you did that, you wouldn't have any friends at all!

I like what Howard F. Lyman, the author of the best-selling book *Mad Cowboy*[1] says, "Don't tell people what you are doing unless they ask, and when they ask, you have thirty seconds to respond. That's about how long their attention lasts. If they want to know more they will research on their own or ask more."

---

1. Lyman, Howard with Metzer, Glen: "Mad Cowboy, Plain Truth From the Cattle Rancher Who Won't Eat Meat." Simon & Schuster, New York, 1998.

Occasionally, people make fun of me for eating raw food, but they're not usually too hard-core. They never say anything like, "You're stupid." They'd rather make fun of me gently, like, "Have some milk. Oh, I forgot, you can't have that because you're crazy." I just respond with, "Yeah, I am crazy. A crazy raw fooder that is! I only eat fruit." When they hear how I start making fun of myself, they lose interest.

In Ashland, people know me as the fruit boy. I just laugh with them. I'm not afraid to make fun of myself! I am healthy and happy, and I don't care what people think. It's only thoughts.

Valya:

I know that I would not be the same person I am today if I hadn't changed my diet. Before going on raw foods, I was failing every subject in third grade except art. I couldn't read, so naturally I couldn't write. Learning geography was out of the question; I was quite happy in Denver, Colorado. History? Yeah, right. That would really come in handy. Who cares about a bunch of dead guys? I was under the impression that THEY were going to teach me without my having to do anything. I had a hard time concentrating and could not remember anything. Fact: to learn, one must have the ability to remember. My energy would bounce from so high that I would be racing through the house back and forth, to so low that I wouldn't have the energy to change the channel on the remote control.

Before I went on raw food, I had asthma. Like many other sicknesses, asthma is considered incurable. I had trouble breathing at night and could not sleep. Whenever I ran, I felt like I was suffocating. My nose was always clogged, and I was pale no matter how much time I spent outside. My health was getting worse. My favorite foods were milk and cheese. (This could be the reason my asthma got so bad). I used to cut a two-inch-thick slice of cheese, put it between some wonder bread, and eat it. Sometimes I'd eat the cheese without the bread. My family would go through two gallons of milk a day. My mother bought six gallons of milk at a time so that it would last for a while. My father was capable of eating three chickens in one sitting. At the age of nine, Sergei could eat an extra-large pizza all by himself! As you can imagine, we were all overweight. The doctors discovered that Sergei had juvenile diabetes, my dad had hyperthyroid, and my mother had a bad heart condition.

Health, however, was far from being my biggest problem. I was unhappy. I tried to entertain myself with movies, restaurants, and theme parks, but pleasure could never fill my empty feeling inside.

My life was slowly zipping by. Every day was just like the day before. I would often wonder where all the time went. It seemed rather fast, as if something was missing. I dreamed of adventure and doing exciting things, but it all seemed pretty hopeless. I was going to get held back in school. As soon as I went on raw food, I switched to home schooling and started learning about the things I wanted to learn about. My grades started going way up.

Learning became exciting for me. I learned by following my curiosity. I found that I was full of questions. It felt like a curtain had been lifted. My brain was filled with a sharp clarity. I began to remember things so much more easily. My energy became balanced. I could sit down and study now. Reading became my favorite thing to do. I understood that I was the only one who could really teach me anything. I saw thousands of opportunities, like doors in front of me, and I became aware that I had to open them myself because no one could do that for me. I stopped expecting to grow up some far off day and suddenly knew what I wanted to do with my life. I realized that I already was the person I was going to be for the rest of my life. My life had already begun!

Before I went on raw food, I had a hard time breathing, especially in spring. When my first "raw" spring came, I was suddenly aware I could breathe through my nose! Many of my friends had colds, runny noses, and allergies. I used to have all of those, and I now had nothing! At that moment, I felt that all my suffering with food cravings was worth it. I realized that I wanted to eat raw foods for the rest of my life.

After I changed my diet, I never had another asthma attack. I lost some weight and started running in the mornings with my brother. I even got to the point where I could whistle while running! Raw food has changed my life. It has made me a healthier person. When a person is healthy, it's easier to be happy.

My life is definitely easier than it would have been if I had not changed my diet. I don't ever need to worry about being sick with any of the thousands of diseases, viruses, or infections. I do not need braces, glasses, or Ritalin. I don't have headaches, toothaches, earaches, colds, allergies, acne, parasites, ADD, (Attention Deficit Disorder) anorexia, or obesity. Sometimes I feel guilty that I'm not sick because I have nothing to relate with other teenagers about. My friends like to talk about their symptoms and I have nothing to say!

Last week I went to the dentist. He was so surprised. He told me that I had some of the best teeth he had ever seen in a teenager.

Sergei:

Back when I was nine years old, my sister and I would talk to each other about the day we turned eighteen. This day would be a special day because on this day, we would stop eating raw food. We would dream about what kind of food we would break the diet with. Corndogs, pizza, nachos, and crab were just some of the foods we were going to order on that magical day.

As the years went by, this dream seemed less and less appetizing until one day when I forgot about it altogether. I started noticing that food did not run my life as before. No longer did my whole existence revolve around it. Spending less time eating gave me more free time during the day. I began using this time for observing others and myself. I noticed how my mother, who worked sixteen-hour days, would have a huge pile of dishes waiting for her at the end of the day, or how my father, who some days did twelve massages in a row, would still have to wash the floor in the kitchen before he passed out. I observed how I felt when I just sat around watching TV while my parents worked and I pretended like I didn't notice.

I still remember the day I made up my mind to wash the dishes for my mom and the floor for my dad. It was the first time in my life that I didn't try to get away with doing as little as possible. I turned on the radio to my favorite station, put on some gloves, and washed those dishes until I could see my reflection in them. The floors always seemed to me like a lot of hard and dirty work, but they were surprisingly easy to do! The reward for me came when my parents, who were so used to washing the dishes and floor, came into the kitchen and found that everything was already done. It was like someone zapped them with a stun gun. It was such an incredible feeling that I decided to help them out more often.

It was that day that I had my first major revelation: I, Sergei Boutenko, enjoyed helping people! I felt good inside every time I helped someone, so I naturally started doing it more often. Once again, I learned how things in life are not always as they seem. When I avoided work and tried to get happiness from entertainment, I was unhappy. When I began working to help others, I was no longer as bored and I became happy.

When I was a year and a half into raw foods, I experienced some profound tooth regeneration. I had thought, "Wow, I'm natural. I don't need to do anything. My teeth will take care of themselves". So I stopped brushing them. After all, dogs didn't brush their teeth. Later, after eating a lot of fruit, I noticed the beginning of cavities. I thought, "Hey, what am I doing wrong? I'm a raw fooder! This is not supposed to happen."

I started looking at my diet and doing research. I came to the conclusion that eating fruit is okay, but it is important to rinse my mouth with water after I eat fruit. After eating dried fruit, I always brush my teeth.

Being almost eighteen, I recently went to the dentist to check on my wisdom teeth. He was amazed that all four of my wisdom teeth were growing perfectly straight. I was overjoyed to hear that I would not need to get my teeth pulled. I consider myself very lucky that I met this special dentist. Dr. Alfred Fosdal, DDS, PC. The fact is that Dr. Fosdal is a raw foodist! He is eighty-three-years young and still a practicing dentist. Dr. Fosdal has been working as a dentist all his life, and he has profound knowledge and understanding about teeth. Dr. Fosdal also taught me some essential procedures for keeping my teeth healthy. He said, "Brush your gums hard! Brush them so hard that your toothbrush bends. Healthy gums will fight harmful bacteria and make your teeth stronger." I am finding that eating more green leafy vegetables and drinking green juice (I drink wheat grass every day) is definitely helping my teeth. My diet now consists of lots of greens, organic ripe fruits, and very little fats. I understand that oils don't exist in nature. Avocados, nuts, and seeds are wonderful and healthy; however, I have noticed that I feel the best when I limit my intake of them.

Valya:

When I was eight, communicating with other people was always difficult. I was afraid to be sincere because I thought I was not good enough and no one would like me. I had to think about what to say. I talked about "safe" things like the weather and the news. I was comfortable speaking with little children, but still we only talked about movies and games. My conversations were always boring because I was shy of my own opinion. I would wait to hear what the other person would say so that I could agree. When I went on raw foods, I became calmer and more sensitive to myself and others. I started enjoying deeper conversations. By talking with other people, I found many feelings inside myself that I hadn't known before. This transformation happened not only to me but to several others as well.

I laugh when I remember how frightened we would get when my mom would say she wanted to talk to us. This was a very bad sign! She usually talked to us only when we "deserved" it. Since we've gone on raw food, our sincere family discussions have become pleasant and often. We frequently sit down and talk to each other for hours. We share about how we feel and what happened in our day. Now I find it easy to talk to other people. I can walk up to anyone and start talking about any subject. I feel that I can relate to anybody.

Sergei:

If I hadn't started eating raw food, I would be like any other "regular" kid except I would be fat, and I would have diabetes. At nine, I was already getting depressed and bored. I always wanted to be entertained, and I noticed that no matter how many movies I watched, I still didn't feel happy. Sometimes I thought, "Why are we here on this earth? There's nothing for us to do here." I was heading in a direction all kids head at some point. Death scared me, so I didn't want to die, but living was boring.

When my family and I moved to Michigan, there was even less to do. No TV, no movie theater, no entertainment at all. Just a little town surrounded by cornfields. I thought, "I hate Michigan. It's so boring here." But life was still going on, and I had to learn how to be with myself. For the first time in my life, I had lots of time, and instead of spending it entertaining myself, I started observing people and nature. I watched how ordinary people around me worked and rested and communicated. They noticed me and asked me questions. At first, I avoided talking to them because these town people and their lives seemed very boring to me. I felt depressed even from looking at them. Later I got into long conversations with these people and started enjoying it. I noticed how much all of us could learn if we talked sincerely. I managed to connect with all people whether children, adults, or college students. I was even fortunate enough to talk to people whose doctors had basically pronounced them dead. That's when real learning started.

In a matter of weeks, I was no longer missing any of my favorite entertainment. I discovered that no one but myself could truly entertain me. That time in Michigan changed my whole perspective on life.

When we started to live in Ashland, I once again gained access to TV, bowling, videogames, movies, and many other modern city pleasures. But now I found them boring and preferred deep conversations, walking in nature, or even working. I had learned so much about myself, and found that I could have fun anywhere. I felt that even if I were stranded on an uninhabited island, I could still live my life and make my days meaningful.

I'm seventeen now, and this is my third year in college. When I found out that I didn't need to go to high school to get into college, I thought, "Why go?" Everybody knows that thirty-six transferable college credits, or a GED, are equal to a high school diploma, and to enter college one doesn't need a diploma at all. I went to the community college and took the placement test. It was surprisingly easy. Although one question that really stumped me was, "How many husbands did Kathleen Turner have?" I failed that one.

I remember turning thirteen years old. My hormones started acting up, and I started growing hair in places where there was none before. All of my friends who went with me to D.A.R.E, and who swore they would never take drugs, went off and got high. On the outside it seemed like they just wanted to be cool and get acceptance by having something in common with other kids, but when I looked at it closer, I saw that this was not accurate. I think maybe they simply realized they were unhappy and that life would be more pleasant if they got happy. It's no wonder that one of the slang words for getting high is "getting happy." It seemed that all my friends were trying to find themselves, but instead they were actually getting further and further away from the truth. I realized that they could not stop getting high even if they wanted to.

I turned down drug offers on a daily basis. I am thankful that I live in a small town because it wasn't long before word got out that I was clean and the offers stopped. It was great because even when occasionally an out-of-towner would offer me a little something, before I could even open my mouth someone would yell, "You're wasting your time. That's Sergei and he's clean."

As a teen, I have chosen to stay away from drugs. Not because my mommy told me they are bad, but because I can see with my own two eyes they are bad for me. Only unhappy people take drugs. This is true because drugs cause a temporary state of happiness. Since I am already happy, it would not make any sense for me to spend money on something that I already possess.

I notice how much potential kids my age have, and how much they are wasting on drugs. I've watched some of my friends transform from being bright happy people, ready to help or go places, into people who just sit on the couch by their TV all day long, calling their friends and saying, "Wow, man, I'm so high." I witness how drugs make everybody unmotivated. When I think about my generation, which is the future of the world, this thought brings me down. I feel so sad! I see how many kids are into drugs. If they're just going to be killing, dulling, and numbing themselves, then I don't know where we are going to end up.

This summer at our Raw Teen Hike, I met eighteen kids who eat raw food. They are between fifteen and eighteen years old. I was amazed how much some of them had accomplished. It seemed like they lived seven lives. Even those that hadn't done many things had still accomplished a lot because they had achieved happiness. To me, food is not the most important thing in life. When I meet people I never think, "Oh, you eat meat, I can't be friends with you." However, healthy food gives us the energy to be healthy and happy. When we eat food with energy, we become people with energy. The difference between people with energy and people without energy is quite dramatic. I have noticed that I am more attracted to people who are healthy and happy. I think happiness is the most important goal in life. Even if I had a PhD, a mansion in Hawaii with a private swimming pool, and all the cars and money I wanted, if I was unhappy, all the riches in the world would count for nothing.

In the past I have seen a few of my girlfriends take drugs. I saw what those drugs did to their physical bodies and the complications they acquired. Moreover, I saw the hidden damage those drugs did to their spiritual beings, and I must say that was the worst. Beautiful, young, lively women became numb, indifferent, and unattractive. It was not enjoyable to hang out with them anymore. I find raw girls more interesting.

Valya:

The biggest change I noticed from going on raw food is that I gained much mental clarity. I was amazed to discover that I can understand every subject. I'm sixteen and in college now. It's easy for me to write essays now for my writing class. I can just sit down and say exactly how I feel on paper. Several times my teacher has asked if I've had help or if I've written it myself.

I notice that many grownups don't have much clarity and their thoughts get confused. In their essays, they don't talk about how they feel. Instead, they describe what happens. Feelings are very important. They are the most fun to write about and the most fun to read about, because the reader can often relate to the author's feelings.

I used to have a horrible memory and, in school, that's the worst thing one could have. I would daydream a lot. I always got into trouble for forgetting things. I couldn't spell because I couldn't remember how to spell. I couldn't memorize math or science formulas. When I went on raw foods, I suddenly started remembering things.

I have also discovered so much more patience! Before I went on raw food, I was not able to sit down and read a book for more than fifteen minutes. I couldn't sit for that long. Once I began eating raw food I started to love to read so much that I could read a book for five solid hours, cover to cover. My mom would have to pry my cold hands off of the thing.

Switching to a raw food lifestyle and staying on it when most people around me were eating cooked food was not easy. It made me stronger. Now I know I can do anything in my life. I can accomplish any goal. I believe that others too can achieve anything they want. If you choose to do what you love, you can be very successful.

I've noticed at my college that a lot of students go into computers just to make money. They don't even like computers. They say, "I hate my major. I hate doing what I'm doing." Once they finish their education, they are going to be stuck with their chosen profession and there's no way these people are going to be content with their life because they can't stand what they're doing.

I am going to do something great with my life. Everyone has this chance and I don't want to miss it. When I die, I will have left this world a little better than it was when I got here. I know that because I am in charge of my life. No amount of hard work can stop me. Raw food helped me to make my highest dreams become possible.

Sergei:

In my family, we are all equal. We make decisions together. As kids, we are not excluded. I think that's important because knowing how to make decisions is useful in life. I am not afraid to share my thoughts and feelings with my parents. I am sad and amazed that many of my friends have a habit of hiding their lives from their parents. I feel lucky that in my family we can talk about any problem. And when we don't have a problem, we still talk.

When we make a decision, everyone takes part. For example, once our friend said, "Your family is going on a four-month trip. I know how hard it is to travel in a van, so I'm going to give you my RV for free. You don't have to pay me anything." Our mom and dad got excited and said, "This is awesome!" Then we went for a ride in the

RV. It was old and big. Our parents asked our opinion "Well, should we take it? Do you want to ride in it?" I said, "No, I'd rather ride in the van because the RV is big and bulky, and one would need to be a mechanic if something broke on the road, and none of us are. We don't want to be stuck somewhere." My sister agreed, and then our parents thought about it and decided not to accept this seemingly great offer.

Valya:

We have complete freedom in our family. Usually my mother doesn't have to ask, but if she asks me to wash the dishes, I know that as a human being I have the right to say no. I know that I could refuse and that would be perfectly fine. But I never do, because I love my mom and want to lighten her load.

Sergei:

Parents, I know you want to help your children become healthier, happier people. Unfortunately, I see that many parents' sincere efforts aren't successful. I want to share with you the main thing my parents did that helped me be raw. They stayed on raw food themselves! I think that children subconsciously copy their parents. In nature, a mother bear teaches her cubs what to eat by placing certain berries or roots in her mouth, chewing them up, and then showing her cubs. I believe that we humans still have some instincts left in us. It is essential that your kids see you eating healthy food before they make the shift for themselves. Kids don't like when their parents tell them not to eat pizza while doing it themselves. I'm so grateful to my parents for helping me to change my diet.

It is crucial to explain to your kids why you are going raw. Put yourself in your child's place. How would you like raw foods to be introduced to you? Would you like to be forced to eat what at first seems to be un-tasty, unattractive food for some unknown reason? Forcing children will only turn them away from raw food. Take some time and explain why this diet is important. Let them make their own choice.

What makes going on raw food so difficult? By changing to raw food, you will go against the main-stream! In the beginning, such a radical change creates many uncomfortable and unfamiliar social situations. Children are especially sensitive to them. You cannot expect them to thrive in mainstream surroundings alone. Spending more time with your kids will enable their adjustment to their new lifestyle. I remember how I needed my parents' support in the beginning. I appreciated the hikes and long conversations we had together. We discussed life, death, and everything in between.

Enrolling your kids into different fun classes such as swimming, horseback riding, fencing, etc., will divert their attention from the emotional pressure during the transition.

A good way to get information to your child about the benefits of raw food is through "subliminal" messages. My mom used to copy jokes onto separate pieces of paper and hang them up around the house. It's funny that this worked best in the bathroom because while sitting on the pot I had nothing to do so, I was forced to read them. After about a month of switching jokes my mother replaced them with raw food quotes and excerpts from different health books. Now I was the one telling her, "Did you know that every can of soda pop has 11 tea-spoons of sugar in it?" and "Did you know that sugar is a drug?" My mom would just smile and say "OK, honey, I won't buy you any pop from now on."

Another thing that helped me was that my parents taught me at an early age how to use all the basic raw food equipment. At some garage sale, they bought me my own real blender, food processor, and dehydrator. Knowing how to use these tools gave me an opportunity to create my own raw dishes and practice my own form of art. My parents made raw foods an adventure for me. To this day, a big part of enjoying what I eat is the fact that I make it myself.

For smaller children, collecting fruit works as a great incentive to eat healthier. Buy two fruit charts, a sub-tropical and a tropical. Every week buy a fruit from the chart and enjoy it with your child. You don't need to live on Maui to eat exotic fruit. Check your local Asian market where you will find all kinds of tropical fruit at reasonable prices. This will make eating raw fun while educating your child about the diverse world of fruit. Fruit is more than just apples, oranges, and bananas.

Warning: Packing exotic fruit in your child's school lunch will make them popular at school. Other kids may get excited by the look and taste of dragon fruit, durian, and jackfruit and may even try to take it away. In the long run, you may go bankrupt trying to feed the whole elementary school!

Valya:

Children, help your parents to be healthy! Encourage their feeble attempts at making energy soup. Drink wheat grass juice every morning with them. They won't do it

without you. You can't even imagine how much your
opinion matters to them.

I didn't know that I was sick until I became healthy.
I didn't know that I was sad until I became happy. Who
would have thought that something as small as my diet
could change my life so much! I realize that if we do not
change our diets, we will all get sick. It is inevitable.
How many completely healthy people do you know?
Let us not wait until we have no other choice.
Sometimes we try to take the easy way out. There is no
easy way. There is only the hard way, and the harder
way. We only get one chance to live each moment. Let
us never miss a chance to change or do something better right now, because this is the only now we have.

I've met several kids who have gone on raw foods
and their families haven't. I think it's difficult when the
whole family isn't on raw foods. I am amazed that they
not only keep staying on raw food but also get their parents into it. The parents see their children as the example, and then they go on raw foods. I think staying on
raw food is especially hard for children who do it on
their own. I cannot even imagine how difficult it is,
because I've grown up in a family that eats raw food. I
know a sixteen-year-old girl name Jackie from
Baltimore. She is the only one in her family who eats
raw food. The rest of the family cooks their food. She
sits down to eat with them having only a salad, and it's
so wonderful that her parents cooperate with her and
don't say things like, "You're going to become anorexic;
you're going to die, we've got to take you to a psychol-
ogist, you have a problem."

If you are a teenager, I think raw food is worth a try.
Even if you can't do it while you're still living with your

parents, it's a good idea to have in your mind so that maybe at another time and place you can be raw.

Sergei and Valya:

Staying on raw food is difficult but possible. Having a support group is very helpful. We put together a teen hike in 2002 that was highly successful. We are planning to have two or three hikes every year. We have put together a raw teen e-group! We believe that it is very important for the youth of the world to start thinking about the future. Why? Because we *are* the future. Our parents and our grandparents will not be around forever. Time flies and soon we will have to step up and take care of our lives and our planet.

Guys, girls! If we don't want to spend our lives living in huge polluted cities and raising our future children with color pictures of what trees used to look like, we've got to start acting today. Through the raw teen e-group, we hope to unite teens together and discuss how we can make our own lives and futures better. To subscribe to the raw teen e-group, please email us! Our emails are Sergei@rawfamily.com and Valya@raw family.com. In addition, we have a new web site www.sergeiandvalya.com, which describes teen events and experiences with raw food.

Sergei and Valya's Photo Album

Photo by Katherine@3rdEyeFoto.ca

When my sister and I prepare food together we inspire and learn from one another. Valya helps me decorate a cake. I help her figure out what's missing in her soup. We have a natural sort of flow! Together we are able to create art fit for kings.

With this picture section we wanted to share with you how raw food enriches our lives.

We welcome you to our raw world!

Photo by Katherine@3rdEyeFoto.ca

Unicycling helps us to balance our lives.

Photo from family archive

We love to swim in ice cold rivers year round.

Photo from family archive

Valya grows many beautiful plants.

Photo by Katherine@3rdEyeFoto.ca

Sergei likes to eat what Valya grows!

Photo by Katherine@3rdEyeFoto.ca

Getting a new angle on life!

Sergei is teaching a cooking class.

Valya has a lot to share.

Photo by Katherine@3rdEyeFoto.ca

I enjoy a close friendship with my mom.

Photo by Libby Frost

United we stand!

Photo from family archive

Raw teen hike 2002.

Photo from family archive

GO RAW TEENS!

Photo from family archive

Raw nut loaf made with live garden burger.

Photo by Lorie Neeser, Exposures Photography

Mushrooms stuffed with pecan paté.

Photo by Lorie Neeser, Exposures Photography

Raw finger food: Igor's flax crackers with
nut paté and Greek olives.

Photo from family archive

Psyllium pudding is excellent for breakfast.

Delicious live morning cereal.

Un-chocolate cake decorated with white coconut cream.

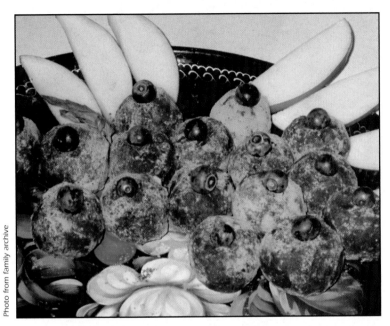

Sergei's amazing truffles.

Un-chocolate cake.

Sergei's coconut dream cake.

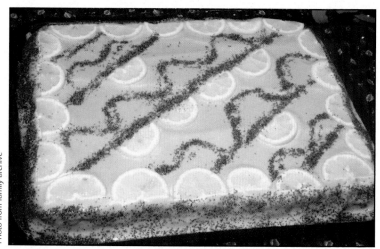

Lemon poppy seed cake.

Apple cranberry sauce.

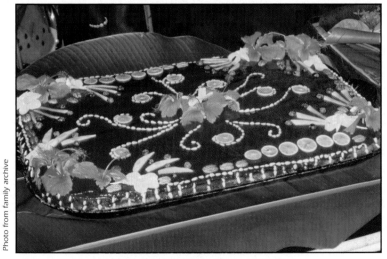

Monster un-chocolate cake for
260 guests at raw event in Jamaica.

Photo from family archive

Live Rawssian borscht.

Photo from family archive

Live pizza.

Photo from family archive

Nut loaf served with gazpacho.

Photo from family archive

Walnut cream cake.

Wedding cake.

Part One
Savory Foods

When we started eating raw food, we wanted to eat things that reminded us of cooked food. It was easier to stay on the diet when we enjoyed our food. Raw gourmet food is the food you eat when you are in the transition period between cooked food and raw food. This is "party" food that you serve for your friends at special events in your life. The longer you stay on raw food, the less you will enjoy eating gourmet raw food. You will eventually notice how you prefer to eat more simply. Naturally, without forcing yourself, your body will let you know that it prefers whole fruits and vegetables over gourmet food. Though we almost never eat raw gourmet food any more, we still enjoy preparing it for others. Eating wholesome food is not the only way to benefit. When we make our food we try being positive and putting our love into the food. The quality of the food automatically goes up. Now, instead of just feeding people healthy, organic, raw food, we also include healthy and wholesome, unconditional love and raw energy. This may be even healthier than the nutrients in the food! Raw gourmet food is an art that we love; we may get tired of eating it at times, but we never get tired of creating it.

One

How We Make Our Food Tasty

The Balance of Five Tastes

Can raw food be as tasty as cooked food? Absolutely! We have learned how to prepare very delicious raw food, and our family has been successfully teaching secrets of raw gourmet dishes to hundreds of men and women of different ages. During the last few years, we have simply stopped telling people that our food is raw unless they ask.

There is a principal difference between cooking a meal and preparing live food. In the cooked dishes, sugar is always sugar, flour is always flour, and salt is always salt. In the raw world, no two lemons are alike. One is bigger and has more juice; the other one has thick skin and is more sour. You could do the same recipe, measure carefully, follow every step, and still it would turn out different each time because of the variables inherent in live food. Cooked corn, cooked zucchini, cooked peas, and other cooked vegetables taste almost the same and require, at the least, oil and salt

■ 39 ■

added. Raw corn, zucchini, peas, and other raw vegetables all have their own unique taste that is impossible to confuse.

When we prepare a raw dish, we use recipes only as ideas, as general guidelines, or just for the ingredients. Then we adjust the final taste using a method of five tastes. There are thousands of different tastes in natural food, but when we balance five major ones, the food is so delicious that everyone says, "Wow!" These five tastes are: sweet, sour, salty, spicy, and bitter. When you learn to balance the five tastes, you will make delicious food. When all five groups of taste buds on your tongue are excited, you *will* say, "Wow!"

When you attempt to un-cook a delicious meal, make sure that all five tastes are present in the final taste and not one is missing. Each of the five tastes doesn't have to be strong, but just enough for a particular dish. For example, the strongest tastes in a garden burger should be sweet, spicy, and salty with only a touch of sour and bitter, but all five need to be present. Otherwise, the garden burger will taste bland.

After several months of eating raw food, you will start to notice that more and more often you prefer to eat whole food rather than prepared. In fact, all whole foods, if they are ripe, already naturally have the most balanced bouquet of tastes. However, the taste of natural food is so delicate that unfortunately, after many years of consuming cooked food filled with condiments, our taste buds can no longer enjoy natural flavors. That is why we need a transition time.

Following is a list of suggested ingredients for the five taste groups. This is only a fraction of what is available on planet Earth. Many plants possess different tastes but have one or two that are more dominant. You have to apply common sense and not add vanilla to the soup or garlic to the candy. Please be creative, these are just ideas for you.

- For sour taste add: lemons, cranberries, rhubarb, lemon grass, sour grass, sorrel, tomatoes, rejuvelac, nut or seed yogurt, or apple cider vinegar.

- For sweet taste add: dry fruit such as figs, dates, prunes, raisins; fresh fruits such as ripe banana, mango, peach, pear; apple juice, orange juice, raw honey, or fresh stevia leaves.

- For spicy taste add: garlic leaves or cloves, onion leaves or bulbs, ginger, mustard greens or seeds, radish, horseradish, cayenne pepper, wasabe sea weed, herbs, fresh or dry such as basil, dill, cilantro, rosemary, cinnamon, nutmeg, vanilla, or peppermint.

- For salty taste add: celery, cilantro, dill, parsley, or sea vegetables such as dulse, kelp, nori, arame, or celtic sea salt.

- For bitter taste add: parsley, celery tops, endive, garlic, onion, dandelion, bay leaf, sage, poultry seasoning, or cayenne pepper.

Comparison of Cooking and Preparing

Ingredients in cooked food always change their initial taste as a result of cooking.	Ingredients in raw food never change their initial taste.
Cooked food has pale unattractive colors and textures.	Raw food is very colorful and naturally appealing to human eyes.
The original rich flavors of raw fruits, vegetables, nuts and seeds disappear almost completely after being heated.	The original rich flavors of raw fruits, vegetables, nuts and seeds stay in the food after preparing without heating.
Plain cooked food is tasteless, requiring enhancement with salt, pepper, and other condiments.	Raw food is naturally delicious and requires very little or no condiments.
The taste of cooked food is determined by condiments.	The taste of raw food is determined by a bouquet of tastes of main ingredients.
Condiments have permanent taste.	Raw fruits, vegetables, nuts and seeds have wide spectrums of tastes.
When making cooked food, to follow a recipe is the most important.	When preparing a raw dish, following a recipe doesn't guarantee a delicious result. You need to always adjust the final taste.

Two

Appetizers

What is an Appetizer? An appetizer is an appetite teaser! An appetizer is what you wish your whole meal could consist of when you go to a restaurant. The purpose of appetizers is to initiate excitement towards food prior to a big meal. Appetizers are little bite-size dishes prepared with bright colors and contrasting tastes. Anything can be an appetizer if served in a small quantity and decorated with color. Marinated and pickled foods work great as appetizers! Just remember, quantity and appeal is everything.

Ideas for Appetizers:

- Stuff paté, garden burger, or marinated foods into the following veggies: tomatoes, bell peppers, celery, onion boats, mushrooms, or hollowed-out cucumbers.

- Serve small portions of crackers with seed cheese.

- Create sushi (Cut nori rolls into 1-inch thick slices.)

- Put together cute mini wraps (Wrap patés and/or marinated mushrooms into cabbage, lettuce, nori sheets, soft crackers, kale, etc.)

- Serve mini soups or sauces in hollowed out vegetables or fruit. For example, bell peppers, lemons, tomatoes, squashes, etc.

- Always decorate appetizers with bright-colored veggies, herbs, or edible flowers.

Better Butter
We love to serve it on freshly made warm crackers.

$1/2$	cup pine nuts
2	lemons, juiced
2	Tablespoons olive oil
$1/4$	cup water
1	teaspoon sea salt

Blend ingredients well until smooth, add more water if needed. Add 1/2 cup coconut butter. Blend well. Pour into jar. Chill in the freezer.

Three

Salads

Valya's Favorite Salad

This salad is great for people who enjoy simple food.

$1/2$	head thinly sliced white cabbage
1	small avocado
$1/4$	white onion diced
$1/6$	bunch fresh dill, chopped
2	Tablespoons grape seed oil
	A squirt of fresh lemon juice
	And a dash of dulse flakes

Serves 1-2

Sergei's Favorite Salad

This salad is my absolute favorite!
It satisfies my craving for food every time!

1	cup chopped red leaf lettuce
1	medium tomato
1	avocado, peeled and chopped
1	Tablespoon raw tahini
$1/2$	cup arame, soaked for 3 minutes
2	Tablespoons lemon juice

Mix all the ingredients in your favorite bowl until the tahini is evenly spread throughout the salad. Yummy!   **Serves 1 ha ha ha!**

Cauliflower Salad

The contrasting colors of the white cauliflower and green onions make this salad visually appealing.

1	head cauliflower
1/4	cup olive oil
1/4	cup lemon juice
1	bunch green onions
1	bunch cilantro
	Salt to taste

Chop the veggies into a bowl then mix them with the rest of ingredients.   **Serves 3-5**

Beet Salad

This salad makes a nice, colorful side dish.

4	large peeled grated beets
5	cloves garlic, grated
1/4	cup lemon juice
1	teaspoon salt
1/4	cup olive oil

Mix all ingredients in a bowl and decorate with chopped parsley.   **Serves 2-4**

I Can't Believe It's Just Cabbage

This salad is a SSS salad—Super fast,
Super easy, and Super delicious.

1	head white cabbage
1/4	cup olive oil
1/4	cup lemon juice
1	teaspoon salt
1	Tablespoon nutritional yeast

Mix all ingredients in a bowl and decorate with your favorite herb.   **Serves 3-5**

Tomato Supreme

People who don't like a lot of vegetables
usually go for this salad.

7	large chopped tomatoes
1	bunch fresh dill
1/4	cup olive oil
1/4	cup lemon juice
1	small red onion, chopped

Mix in a bowl and serve.   **Serves 3-5**

Liver's Birthday Salad

This salad is a great liver cleanser!

2   bunches dandelions
1   large avocado
1/4   cup lemon juice
1/2   teaspoon salt (optional)

Chop the dandelions and avocado into a bowl, then mix in the rest of the ingredients.   **Serves 2-3**

Bean Salad

This salad is great for adding variety.

1   cup sprouted lentils
1   cup garbanzo beans or chick peas
1   cup radish sprouts
1/4   cup grape seed oil
1/4   cup lemon juice
1/2   teaspoon salt (optional)

Chop the sprouts into a bowl and mix with the remainder of the ingredients.   **Serves 2-3**

Russian Carrot Salad

*This salad is especially good in the fall
when carrots are the best.*

10	large grated carrots
5	cloves grated garlic
1	bunch fresh parsley, chopped
1/4	cup olive oil
1/2	teaspoon salt

Mix ingredients in bowl and serve.   **Serves 3-5**

Thai Salad

*This simple salad is one of our favorites. It always turns
out delicious! Thai salad is a permanent hit at potlucks.*

4	cucumbers
	Juice of 1 lemon
1	bunch dill
1	bunch cilantro
1	medium onion diced
3	teaspoons hot curry powder
1	teaspoon salt (or to taste)
3	Tablespoons honey
1/3	cup olive oil
	The meat of one young coconut diced
1	cup sunflower seeds (soaked for 2 hours)

Peel and slice the cucumbers into thin circles and
transfer to a bowl. Thinly dice meat of coconut. Finely

chop the cilantro and dill and mix with the cucumbers. Add the onion, lemon juice, and olive oil. Finish by adding the rest of the ingredients and mixing well.

Serves 5-8

Onion Salad

This salad is best after it sits for 20-30 minutes and spiciness goes away.

2	large red or white onions
1	bunch basil or dill or cilantro
1/4	cup olive oil
1/4	lemon, juiced
1/2	teaspoon salt (optional)

Mix ingredients in a bowl and serve.

Serves 5-7

Carrot-Basil Salad

Grated carrot brings soft flavor to this combination. Lemon juice keeps the colors bright.

10	large carrots, grated
1	bunch basil, chopped
1/4	cup olive oil
1/4	cup lemon juice
1/2	teaspoon salt.
5	cloves of garlic (optional)

Mix in a bowl and serve.   **Serves 5-6**

Wrap Salad

*This salad is good when you are truly hungry
and have no intention of spending lots of time
preparing a salad. It is fast and easy to make.*

2	leaves lettuce, chopped or ripped
1	tomato, chopped
1	clove garlic, minced
1	avocado, mashed

Wrap all ingredients into a big, loose cabbage leaf.
Add 1 Tablespoon raw tahini. Sprinkle with dulse
flakes and lemon juice.   **Serves 1**

Kale Salad

*If you leave this salad for a couple of hours, its dressing
will marinate the kale leaves and make them tender.*

2	bunches curly kale, chopped
1	bunch radishes, thinly sliced
$1/2$	head cauliflower, diced
$1/2$	head white cabbage, sliced
$1/2$	cup olive oil
$1/4$	cup apple cider vinegar
1	teaspoon salt
2	Tablespoons honey or anything else sweet: apple juice, date paste, etc.

Mix all the vegetables in a bowl. Add in the remain-
ing ingredients and mix well.   **Serves 7-9**

Tomato Salad

*This salad has a great texture. Tomatoes make it juicy,
celery makes it crunchy, and avocado makes it smooth.*

7	large tomatoes, chopped
1	large avocado, chopped
1/2	bunch celery, chopped
1/4	cup olive oil
1	teaspoon salt

Mix in a bowl and enjoy!   **Serves 3-5**

Side Salad

Very colorful and tasty!

2	ripe tomatoes
1	bunch parsley, chopped
1	Tablespoon olive oil
	Pinch of salt (optional)

Slice tomatoes. Sprinkle lots of chopped parsley on
top. Drizzle with oil and add a pinch of salt.

Serves 1-2

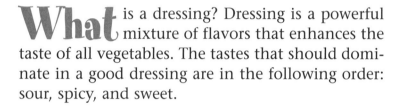

Four

Delicous Dressings

What is a dressing? Dressing is a powerful mixture of flavors that enhances the taste of all vegetables. The tastes that should dominate in a good dressing are in the following order: sour, spicy, and sweet.

Generic Recipe for Dressing

We have come up with all of our best dressings using this generic recipe. With a little practice, anyone can become a dressing master.

Blend the following in a blender until smooth:

> Oil (any good oil such as sesame, olive, safflower). Use enough to cover the blades of the blender.

1	teaspoon honey (or any other natural sweetener, like raisins or banana)
2	Tablespoons fresh lemon juice (or lime juice or apple cider vinegar)
1/3	cup water

1   cup chopped or 1 bunch herbs—preferably
      fresh! (One or a combination of celery, parsley,
      cilantro, basil, or any other)

      Spice to taste (garlic, mustard, ginger,
      jalapeno, etc.)

1/3   cup seeds or nuts (the most common are
      sunflower seeds and tahini; also: walnuts,
      pumpkin seeds, almonds, etc.)

1/2   teaspoon salt (sea salt, kelp, dulse, Bragg's
      Liquid Aminos) to taste, or no salt at all

Don't be afraid to improvise. You may sometimes
add more liquid, or skip one ingredient completely. If
it tastes good, put it in. Good luck!   **Serves 7-10**

Sweet and Sour

*This dressing is very light and is best on hot
summer days. It won't weigh you down.*

1 1/2   cups water
1/2   bunch basil
3-4   Tablespoons honey
1-2   teaspoons salt
1   large ripe tomato
1/4   cup lemon juice
3-4   cloves of garlic

Blend in a blender until smooth!   **Serves 6**

Tahini Dressing

This dressing is so simple that Valya started making it when she was nine.

1	cup water
1/4	cup olive oil
1/4	cup lemon juice
1	Tablespoon raw tahini
4	cloves garlic
1	teaspoon salt

Blend well in blender. (Note: to make it more liquidy, add more water.)   **Serves 6**

Light Tomato Dressing

Tomatoes give this dressing a nice creaminess different from any other. The texture is not only smooth but also light.

2	large ripe tomatoes
3	sticks celery
	Chili pepper to taste
1/4	cup olive oil
1/4	cup apple cider vinegar or lemon juice
1	teaspoon salt
2	Tablespoons honey

Blend in a blender until smooth.   **Serves 6**

Pecan Dressing
*This is a heavier dressing, rich, creamy,
and guaranteed to fill anyone up!*

$^1/_2$ cup pecan
$^1/_2$ bunch oregano
4   sticks rhubarb
1   Tablespoon honey
1   small jalapeno pepper
$^1/_4$ cup olive oil
1   teaspoon salt

Blend until smooth.   **Serves 6**

Creamy Tomato Dressing
*Fresh veggies are fun to dip into
this delicious dressing.*

$^1/_4$ cup olive oil
2   large tomatoes
$^1/_2$ teaspoon sea salt
$^1/_2$ cup almonds
1   Tablespoon honey
$^1/_4$ cup lemon juice
$^1/_2$ bunch celery or parsley

Blend until smooth.   **Serves 6**

Gravy

This is a wonderful substitute for gravy during the holiday seasons.

2   cups pecans, soaked
2   cups water
$^1/_2$ cup dehydrated onion
1   Tablespoon poultry seasoning
2   Tablespoons extra-virgin olive oil
     Salt to taste

Blend the ingredients thoroughly to a gravy consistency.   **Serves 6**

Pesto Dressing

This dressing is good for dipping things into. Great for parties, gatherings, or potlucks.

$^1/_4$ cup olive oil
5   cloves garlic
$^1/_2$ cup pine nuts
1   bunch fresh basil
$^1/_4$ cup lemon juice
1   teaspoon salt

Blend in a blender thoroughly.   **Serves 4-5**

Coco-Yum

*This light dressing will leave you
feeling cool afterwards.*

Meat from 1 young coconut
1/4   cup olive oil
1/2   cup water
1/3   teaspoon salt
3   stalks celery
1   Tablespoon honey
1/2   medium-hot pepper
1/4   cup lemon juice

Blend thoroughly.   **Serves 6**

Thai Sauce

*This sauce is made for dipping nori rolls or sliced veggies.
Place a little cup of this sauce next to nori rolls
and watch people go wild!*

1/4   cup lemon juice
1/4   cup Nama Shoyu
3   cloves garlic
1/4   cup chopped ginger
1   Tablespoon honey

Blend until smooth and creamy.   **Serves 6**

Five

Soups

What is soup? Unlike juice, soup retains the pulp along with chunks of vegetables. Soup is heavier and more filling than juice. As with all raw foods, it is important not to be afraid to experiment. Next time you want to try to make a new soup, think about what makes a soup. If you want to make a creamy soup, start by blending any kind of nuts with water, then add any kind of spices and veggie chunks. If you want to make a vegetable soup, start by blending oil or avocado with some juicy veggie or fruit, then add spices and texture.

Thai Soup

This soup is fast to make which makes it good for large parties. It's out of this world in taste.

2	peeled cucumbers
2	cups water
1/2	cup walnuts
1/4	cup Nama Shoyu or other raw soy sauce
1/2	fresh spicy pepper
1	teaspoon salt
2	Tablespoons honey

1/4   cup chopped ginger
1/4   cup lemon juice
3   Tablespoons turmeric powder

Blend these ingredients in the blender until smooth.
Add additional ingredients and stir well. Enjoy!

Additional Ingredients:
1   peeled cucumber, sliced thinly
1/2   cup dried mushrooms
1   bunch chopped cilantro

Serves 5

Cream of Celery Soup
*This soup is very inexpensive to make
and extremely delicious.*

1   large bunch celery
4   cups water
1/2   cup olive oil
1/4   cup lemon juice
2   teaspoons honey
       Spicy pepper to taste
1-2   teaspoons sea salt

Blend all ingredients in a blender until fine.
Add:
1   chopped avocado
1   small sweet red pepper, chopped

Serves 6

Sea Vegetable Soup

This soup is excellent for people who miss the taste of fish. The favor of the seaweed is nostalgic.

2	cups almonds
4	cups water
$1/2$	cup olive oil
$1/4$	cup lemon juice
2	Tablespoons raw honey or five dates
3	bay leaves
2	teaspoons sea salt
	Sprinkle with chili pepper to taste

Blend all ingredients in a blender until smooth. Add:

4	nori sheets torn into small squares
3	Tablespoons dulse flakes
$1/2$	cup dry arame

Mix these ingredients into the soup and let sit for 20 minutes   **Serves 3-5**

Borscht

This soup tastes just like real Russian Borscht. It is a great soup for multi-cultural gatherings with different ethnic foods.

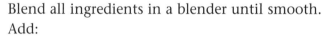

Blend these ingredients well in a blender or Vitamix:

2	cups water
3	beets
1	small root ginger (slice it first)

3-4   large cloves garlic

6-7   bay leaves

Pour the mixture into a big bowl. Blend the following ingredients for a short time (about 30 seconds):

2   cups water

2   carrots

2   stalks celery

2   Tablespoons apple cider vinegar

3-4   oranges, peeled with the seeds out (seeds will make a very bitter taste)

1   Tablespoon honey

1/2   cup olive oil

       Sea salt to taste

Add 1/2 cup walnuts and blend on low speed very quickly so that they break into small pieces but are not blended. Pour in the same bowl and stir.

Dice or grate:

1/4   head cabbage

1-2   carrots

1   bunch parsley

Add grated ingredients to the blended mixture. Stir and serve.   **Serves 7-10**

Generic Recipe for Chowder

If you follow this recipe, you will be amazed at how many different delicious soups you can create on your own.

Blend 1 cup of nuts (soaked overnight) with 2 cups of water. Add 1 cup cashews or walnuts and blend to a creamy consistency. Add the rest of the following and blend well:

1	cup water
1/2	cup extra virgin olive oil
1	teaspoon honey
1	cup chopped celery
	Hot peppers to taste
2-5	cloves garlic
1	teaspoon salt

Now you have plain chowder. You pick the flavor:

For clam-chowder taste add: dulse flakes

For broccoli: chopped broccoli

For mushroom: your favorite mushrooms, dry or fresh

For tomato: chopped tomato

For carrot: grated carrots

For corn: cut corn off the cob or use frozen corn

For pea: fresh or frozen peas

Your own creation . . .

Sprinkle with dry parsley flakes before serving.

Note: this soup will become warm because of much blending. It's still raw. (Just don't let it become hot!) Warm soups are comforting in the cold wintertime.   **Serves 5**

Chili

*This recipe tastes better than real chili
because the beans are not refried!*

Blend the following ingredients in a blender:

1	cup water
2	cups fresh tomatoes, chopped
1/2	cup dates or raisins
1/2	cup extra virgin olive oil
1	cup sun-dried tomatoes
1	cup dehydrated mushrooms
1	cup chopped celery
	Salt or Bragg's Liquid Aminos to taste
1-2	Tablespoons spaghetti seasoning
1-2	Tablespoons juice of lime or lemon
	Hot peppers to taste
2-5	cloves garlic
1	bunch basil

Add 1 pound of bean, pea, or lentil sprouts. Don't blend! Sprinkle with dry parsley flakes before serving.

Note: this soup will become warm because of much blending. It's still raw. (Just don't let it become hot!) Warm dishes are comforting in the cold wintertime.

Serves 5-7

Gazpacho

*This is a great summer dish. It is satisfying
and light. It will not weigh you down
on a hot and muggy summer day.*

Blend the following ingredients in a blender until smooth:

1/2	cup water
1/2	cup extra virgin olive oil
5	large ripe tomatoes
2	cloves garlic or spicy pepper to taste
1	Tablespoon raw honey (dates or raisins work just as well)
1/4	cup lemon juice
1	teaspoon sea salt
1	bunch of fresh basil

Now that you have the gazpacho liquid, cut the following vegetables into 1/2 inch cubes:

1	large avocado
1	medium bell pepper
5	sticks celery
1	small onion

Mix all ingredients in a bowl and sprinkle with chopped parsley.

Serves 4-5

Dill-icious Soup
This is the tastiest summer soup!

Blend together well in a Vitamix:

3	large fresh tomatoes
2-3	cloves garlic
1	bunch dill
1	cup water
1/3	cup lemon juice
1	teaspoon sea salt
$^1/_2$	cup olive oil
$^1/_2$	cup raisins
$^1/_2$	cup dehydrated tomatoes (Add dehydrated tomatoes a little at a time.)

In a bowl, chop avocado, 1 large bell pepper fine.
Mix both sets of ingredients and garnish with dill.

Serves 3-4

Red and Spicy Soup

In a blender, blend:

1-1$^1/_2$ cup	pine nuts
$^1/_2$	cup olive oil
	Juice of $^1/_2$ lemon
6-8	small tomatoes (cherry or other)
6-8	cloves garlic
2	fresh cayenne peppers
1	teaspoon sea salt
$^1/_2$	bunch thyme

Blend well and stir in small chunks of avocado, cucumber, and red and yellow bell pepper. Decorate with chunks of red and yellow peppers!   **Serves 3**

Ruth & McCall's Curry Glory

This soup is delicious and rich in flavor

Blend together:

1	cup water
1	teaspoon curry powder
4	large ripe tomatoes
1	orange and 1 yellow bell pepper
1/4	cup lemon juice
1	teaspoon paprika
1/4	cup olive oil
2	cloves garlic
2	Tablespoons onion powder
2	Tablespoons honey
1	teaspoon salt
1/2	avocado
1/2	cup cauliflower
1	bunch fresh parsley or dill
1/2	teaspoon white pepper

Pour into a bowl and add:

1/4 cup of each: dehydrated tomatoes, mushrooms, and onions. Sprinkle fresh basil and chopped tomatoes (optional) on top.   **Serves 6**

Patrick's Watermelon-Raspberry Soup

The unique balance of spiciness, coolness, and
sweetness makes this a pleasant soup.

Combine and blend:

1/2	watermelon
1	pint raspberries
4	stalks rhubarb
1/2	chili pepper

Serve chilled in hollowed-out watermelon bowl.
Slice a couple of pieces of watermelon and garnish
with edible flowers.   **Serves 6**

"Dill-light-ful" Soup

This quick and easy recipe is very tasty.

Blend:

2	cups coconut water
1	avocado
1	stalk celery
1	stalk rhubarb
1/2	bunch fresh dill

Serve chilled, garnish with dill.   **Serves 4**

Ginger Soup
This soup has a wonderful gingery punch.

Blend in Vitamix:

1/2	cup pecans
2	cups coconut milk
2	fingers ginger root, sliced
1	bunch fresh basil
1	hot, dried pepper
1/2	teaspoon salt
1/4	cup lemon juice

Place in bowl. Cut up (not blend):

1/2	cucumber
1/2	bell pepper
1/2	avocado
2	Tablespoons dehydrated sweet onion

Garnish with:

    Edible flowers

    Dill

Serves 4-5

Un-Chicken Noodle Soup
*When the potato and dried mushrooms absorb
the liquid, they taste just like chicken.*

Blend together:

2   cups water
1/2   cup walnuts or pecans

Add the following and blend for about 1 minute:
2   cups celery, chopped
2   Tablespoons Nama Shoyu
1   clove garlic
      Pepper to taste, if desired

Pour into a large bowl and add:
1   medium carrot, grated
1/2   bunch parsley, chopped
2   medium, raw potatoes, grated or
      processed with a Spiraliser
      Sliced dried mushrooms (optional)

Serves 7

Six

Entrées

What is an entrée? Why is salad not an entrée? An entrée is usually used as a filler. The ingredients that go into an entrée are heavier than those of a salad because they are usually of a nut or seed base. We can create an infinite variety of different patés and then play with them. For instance if you are tired of eating the same paté plain or with vegetables, try altering the taste by rolling it into nori sheets, making a cabbage wrap, or spreading the paté onto a cracker. Use your imagination!

Live Garden Burger

This recipe is quite possibly the most versatile recipe.
With garden burger you can make nori rolls, cabbage
wraps, spread it on crackers, stuff mushrooms, peppers,
tomatoes, onions, cucumbers, and more.

Grind 1 pound of your favorite nuts in a food processor. Combine the following ingredients and put through a Champion Juicer with the blank plate in or grind in a food processor:

1	pound carrots
1	medium onion

1   Tablespoon sweetener (honey, very
         ripe banana, raisins)
1   Tablespoon oil
1-2   Tablespoons poultry seasoning
         (or other seasoning)
         Sea salt to taste

If the mixture is not firm enough, add one or more
of the following thickeners: dill weed, dried garlic,
dried onion, dried parsley flakes, nutritional yeast,
psyllium husk powder, or ground flaxseeds. Form into
balls, cutlets, or fillets and sprinkle with a little paprika
before serving.

*Note: If you want "fishburger," add seaweed (dulse,
kelp, nori) to the mixture.*   **Serves 10**

Portobello Mushroom Burger
*When finished, Portobello mushroom burgers
look absolutely like real burgers.*

Grind 1 pound of your favorite nuts in a food
processor. Combine the following ingredients and put
through a Champion Juicer with the blank plate in or
grind in a food processor:

1 lb.   carrots
1   medium onion
1   Tablespoon sweetener
         (honey, very ripe banana, raisins)
1   Tablespoon oil
1-2   Tablespoons poultry seasoning
         (or other seasoning)
         Sea salt to taste

If the mixture is not firm enough, add one or more of the following thickeners: dill weed, dried garlic, dried onion, dried parsley flakes, nutritional yeast, psyllium husk powder, ground flaxseeds. Form into 10 burgers. Slice 2 large, ripe tomatoes and 1 large red onion.

Have the following ready:

10 small (or 5 large) Portobello mushroom caps

10 leaves fresh spinach

Assemble mushroom burgers as follows:

Put mushroom cap upside down on a plate, put spinach leaf on it, put burger on spinach, put slice of tomato on burger, put slice of onion on tomato. You may secure your "sandwich" with toothpicks.

Serves 10

Nori Rolls

If you slice the whole nori roll into 1-inch slices, it looks elegant and very appetizing.

Paté mixture:

1/2	cup walnuts
2	cups sunflower seeds, soaked overnight
3	garlic cloves
1	cup chopped celery
1	teaspoon salt
1/3	cup olive oil
1/2	cup lemon juice
1	teaspoon curry powder (or your favorite seasoning)

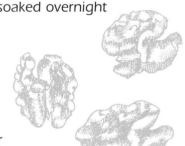

Additional ingredients: Slice into long, thin strips the following:

  1/2   avocado
  1/2   large bell pepper
  2   green onions
  5   raw nori sheets

Blend all the paté ingredients in a food processor until creamy. Spread the paté onto a sheet of nori and add the thinly sliced vegetables. Roll up tight in nori sheet. Note: to make the nori sheets stick better you can moisten them a little with water, lemon, tomato, or orange juice. Let the nori rolls sit for 10 minutes and then begin slicing them into 2-inch slices.

Makes 10-15 nori rolls

Valya's Spicy Almond Cheese

This cheese is great mixed with a salad, on top of crackers, or eaten with celery sticks.

Mix the following ingredients in a bowl:

  2   cups pulp from almond milk
        (pulp should not be sweet)
  1/2   cup olive oil
  1/4   cup lemon juice
  1/2   teaspoon salt
  1/2   bunch fresh or dried dill weed
  1/2   cup diced onions
  1/2   cup diced red bell pepper

Decorate with cherry tomatoes.   **Serves 4**

Live Pizza
*Sergei's friends were very impressed with
this live version of their favorite dish.*

Crust
Grind 2 cups flaxseed in a dry Vita-mix container.
Blend together:

1	cup of water
1	large onion, chopped
3	stalks celery, chopped
2	tomatoes, medium
4	cloves garlic, medium
1	teaspoon Celtic salt

Mix ground flaxseed into blended mix by the
hand. Spread on dehydrating sheets with a spatula.
Divide into squares of desired size. Dehydrate only
until dry, but not crispy.

Topping
Blend the following ingredients with as little water
as possible:

1	pound any nuts
1/2	cup sun-dried tomatoes
1/2	cup raisins
	Juice of 1 medium lemon
2	Tablespoons olive oil
1	Tablespoon dry basil

Pour in a bowl. Add:

1	Tablespoon dry onion

1   Tablespoon dry garlic

2-3   Tablespoons nutritional yeast

1   Tablespoon miso

Mix well.

Making the Pizza

Spread topping on squares of crust.

Decorate with grated yams, sliced cherry tomatoes, sliced mushrooms, sliced olives, and chopped parsley.

Makes nine "slices" of pizza.

Valya's Sunflower Supreme

This savory torte looks very impressive when finished.

4   cups sunflower seeds

1   large white onion

1   bunch Italian parsley

2   cloves garlic

1/4   cup lemon juice

1/4   cup olive oil

1   teaspoon salt

Make a layer of paté on a plate. For the next layer, use sliced tomatoes. Last but not least, spread another layer of paté on top of the tomatoes.

Serves 4-6

Worthy Guacamole
This is a great recipe to dip dehydrated veggie chips into.

Blend the following ingredients in a food processor:

3	large RIPE avocados
1	teaspoon sea salt
1/4	cup lemon juice
4-8	cloves garlic (depending on how much you like garlic)

Chop the following ingredients:

1	medium tomato
1/2	medium onion
1	bunch cilantro

Mix all ingredients in a bowl and sprinkle with chili pepper if desired. Eat on top of crackers. Wrap into cabbage or nori. Fill lettuce or simply eat with a spoon.

Serves 4-6

Better Than Real Burritos
We honestly thought we would never eat anything that resembled a real burrito again until we invented this dish.

Bread
Follow the recipe for Igor's crackers (see Chapter Nine). Dehydrate them only half-way. They will be ready when they feel soft.

Note: the possibilities with soft crackers are endless. You can wrap them around anything, and you can stuff them with anything. So experiment!

Paté

 3   cups almonds
 5-6   cups water

Blend these ingredients in a blender until smooth and strain through a milk bag.

Take the almond pulp and add:

 1/2   cup finely chopped green onion
 1   bunch fresh dill, chopped
 1/4   cup olive oil
 1/4   cup lemon or lime juice
 2   teaspoons sea salt
        Sprinkle with cayenne pepper to taste

Finally: Take your soft cracker and spread as much paté on half of it as you like. Simply roll the paté into the cracker and pin at both ends with a tooth pick!

Un-Spaghetti
Even the color of the noodle strands looks real.

Shred or use vegetable slicer to create thin, noodle-like strands of butternut squash. (If you don't have a slicer, use a grater and make longer strokes.) Sprinkle with paprika and oil before serving. Decorate with fresh parsley.

Tomato-Basil Sauce
This sauce is to live for!

Blend 2 cups fresh chopped tomatoes. Add the following ingredients and blend:

2-4	cloves garlic
1/2	cup chopped fresh basil
	Juice of 1 medium lemon
2	Tablespoons olive oil
4	dates (or some raisins)
1	cup sun-dried tomatoes

Serves 7

Crunch Fries with Ketchup
They look as real as if we got them through the drive-thru window.

Crunch Fries
Slice 1 pound jicama so it looks like French fries. Combine in a bowl with:

1	Tablespoon onion powder
2	Tablespoons extra virgin olive oil
	Sea salt to taste
1	Tablespoon paprika

Ketchup

1/2	cup dried tomatoes, soaked for 2 hours
1/4	cup apple cider vinegar
1/4	cup raisins
1/4	cup onion powder
1	Tablespoon salt

Serves 5

Pecan Paté
This paté has a unique, tender taste.

Mix the following ingredients in food processor until finely chopped:

3 cups raw pecans, soaked overnight
1/2 cup dates
3 cloves garlic (spicy pepper works great)
1/4 cup lemon juice
1/4 cup olive oil
1 bunch fresh cilantro
1 teaspoon sea salt

Use the paté to stuff bell peppers, cabbage leaves, nori rolls, etc. **Serves 5-6 people**

Sunny Spread
This spread is tasty in nori rolls and stuffed peppers.

1/2 cup walnuts
2 cups sunflower seeds, soaked overnight
3 cloves garlic
1 cup chopped celery
1 teaspoon salt
1/3 cup olive oil
1/4 cup lemon juice
1 Tablespoon dry basil

Blend ingredients in food processor until smooth. Be creative and serve on cracker, rolled up in a cabbage leaf, or stuffed in a bell pepper. **Serves 12**

Turkeyless Turkey

We have fun with this dish on Thanksgiving Day.

1/2	pound almonds, soak overnight if possible
1/2	pound walnuts, soak overnight if possible
1	pound carrots, finely grated
1	medium onion, finely chopped
1	Tablespoon raisins
1	Tablespoon oil
1	Tablespoon caraway seeds, ground
1/2	Tablespoon dry ginger, ground
1	Tablespoon Italian seasoning
	Sea salt to taste

Combine all ingredients and put through a Champion Juicer with the blank plate in or mix in a food processor. If the mixture is not firm enough, add one or a couple of the following thickeners: dill weed, dried garlic, dried onion, dried parsley flakes, nutritional yeast, psyllium husk powder, ground flaxseeds.

Form into "drumsticks," sprinkle with paprika or ground black pepper before serving.

Serves 10

Instead of Mashed Potato

If you want to make something quick and yummy,
make this one! We make this dish not only
for Thanksgiving but year round!

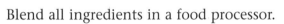

2   large avocados, mashed
1/2 head of cauliflower
1/2 cup lemon juice
1/2 cup sweet onion powder
2   teaspoons sea salt

Blend all ingredients in a food processor.

Serves 6

Stuffing Supreme

One more mandatory dish for the holidays!

1/2 cup soaked sunflower seeds
1-2 teaspoons dill seed
2   teaspoons lemon juice
1   Tablespoon psyllium husk powder
2   teaspoons minced onion
1/4 teaspoon salt

Mix all ingredients in the food processor. Serve
sprinkled with paprika and garnished with parsley.

Yield: 1 cup stuffing

Italian Rawsage

These raw sausages have a delicious nostalgic taste.

1	cup pumpkin seeds
1/2	head of cabbage
1/2	cup olive oil
5	cloves of garlic
1/2	cup onion powder
1	Tablespoon caraway seeds
1	Tablespoon sage, dry
1/2	bunch fresh basil

Blend all ingredients in a food processor. Form into sausage shaped patties.   **Serves 8**

Sergei's Hummus

*Sergei ate this dish every day for a year
and still didn't get tired of it!*

Blend the following ingredients in a food processor:

2   cups garbanzo beans, sprouted for 1 day
1/2   cup extra virgin olive oil
2   chopped carrots
1   cup tomatoes, chopped
1   cup celery, chopped
       Salt or Bragg's to taste
1-2   Tablespoons (dry), or 1 cup (fresh) dill or basil
1-2   Tablespoons lime or lemon juice
       Hot peppers to taste
2-5   cloves garlic

Sprinkle with dry parsley flakes before serving.

Serves 5-7

Seven

Fermented Foods

Fermented foods add a different texture and bright sharp taste to the raw cuisine. Marinated veggies and pickles always make a meal special. We always ferment foods for the holidays. Fermented foods have a lot of acidophilus and vitamin B-12. They are very good for your digestion.

Nut or Seed Yogurt

Tastes much better than dairy yogurt.
Valya loves yogurt with fruit for breakfast.

1 cup any nuts or seeds soaked overnight
1 cup water

Blend nuts with water thoroughly in a blender until smooth. Keep adding water until you have the consistency of heavy cream. Strain mixture through a sprout bag. Pour into a jar and cover with a cheese-cloth for the transfer of air and gases. Set your jar in a warm place where the yogurt temperature can heat up

to 90-100 degrees. It will be ready in approximately 6
to 12 hours or when it tastes tart and sour.

Serves 5

Nut and seed yogurts can be made from sesame
seeds, almonds, pecans, hazelnuts, cashews, sunflower
seeds and any other nuts, seeds, or their combinations.
You may play with the taste by adding a little honey,
lemon juice, sea salt, vanilla, or other flavors. The
longer your yogurt stays in a warm place, the stronger
and sourer it will become.

Suggested combinations for making delicious
yogurt:

Cashew	Sunflower and almond
Cashew and sesame	Pecans and almonds
Cashew, almonds, and sesame	Walnuts and pine nuts
	Sesame and hazelnuts
Cashew and sunflower	
Sesame and almond	

Nut or Seed Cheese

*Sometimes we get tired of patés and garden burgers. This
recipe gives us a different texture with a different taste:*

2 cups any nuts or seeds (soaked overnight)
1 cup water

Soak the nuts and seeds in pure water overnight.
Drain and rinse the nuts and seeds. Put into blender

with one cup of pure water and blend well to break the nuts down into a fine cream. Pour into sprout bag. Hang the sprout bag over a sink or bowl (to pour off the whey) and let ferment at room temperature for approximately 8-12 hours. Transfer cheese to a bowl, mix with your favorite seasonings, and stir well.

Yields 1 pint.

Keeps for at least 7 days in a covered container in the refrigerator. To flavor seed cheese you may use any combination of the following:

Garlic	Chopped or dry dill
Lemon juice	Sun-dried tomatoes
Chopped fresh cilantro	Chopped scallions
Bragg's Liquid Aminos or Nama Shoyu	Basil
Curry powder	Olive oil
Chopped or dry parsley	Sea salt

Marinated Dried Mushrooms

Sergei absolutely prefers this way of marinating mushrooms to any other.

Dry whole mushrooms in dehydrator on Teflex sheets for 24 hours. Put mushrooms in a gallon jar. In Vitamix blend:

1 1/2   cups Namu Shoyu

1   cup olive oil

1   cup lemon juice

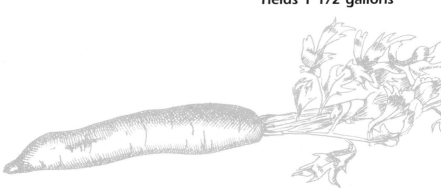

$^1/_4$ cup fresh ginger

3-5   Tablespoons honey

2-4   teaspoons salt

Pour over mushrooms and mix so that all mushrooms are soaked. Soak for a few hours. Can re-use marinade.

Sauerkraut

*This is so delicious that we had to learn
to be careful not to overeat it!*

Grate the following ingredients in bowl:

3   medium heads cabbage

5   carrots

8   bay leaves

1   Tablespoon dill seed

2   Tablespoons salt

Cover the mixture with a plate and something heavy like a container of water to keep the juice coming up. Don't let cabbage dry out on top.

Yields 1 1/2 gallons

Live Kim Chee

*Our dad got through his cooked food cravings
with the help of this recipe.*

In a gallon jar, chop:

2	heads Napa cabbage
1	head bok choy
4	cloves minced garlic
1/2	hot pepper, minced
1/2	cup water
1	Tablespoon salt
2	Tablespoons paprika

Put in Vitamix:

1	Tablespoon honey
1	piece sliced ginger
1/2	cup apple cider vinegar

Blend well, then pour into jar. Press and squeeze
cabbage into jar. Don't cover with lid: put cheesecloth
or something similar so it can breathe. Ferment 3 days
(but can eat after 4 hours), then put in fridge.

Yields 1 gallon

Pickled Zucchini, Eggplant
People who don't like the taste of plain, raw zucchini or eggplant will rave over this dish!

Cut into half-inch slices:

1   eggplant

Cut into one-inch slices:

3-4   medium green zucchini

3-4   yellow zucchini

Put all in gallon jar

Put in Vitamix:

1   cup water

6-8   cloves garlic

2   Tablespoons salt

2   Tablespoons honey

1   bunch fresh oregano

1   bunch fresh thyme

1/2   cup apple cider vinegar

Pour everything into jar and mix by hand. Cover with cloth. Let sit for 3 days.   **Yields 1 gallon**

Marinated Mushrooms

Put in gallon jar:

3 lbs shitake, crimini, or regular button
white mushrooms

Blend in Vitamix:

1   cup lemon juice or apple cider vinegar

1   Tablespoon honey

1   bunch fresh basil

$1/2$ cup olive oil

2   Tablespoons salt

1   cup water

1   chili pepper

Pour into jar over mushrooms. Marinate 1 day.

Yields 1/2 gallon

Cranberry Apple Relish

3   cups fresh cranberries

2   medium apples, cored & quartered

1   medium pear, cored & quartered

$1^{1/2}$ cups raisins

1   cup apple juice

$1/2$ cup nuts

$1/2$ lemon with peel but without seeds

Blend all ingredients in a food processor until finely chopped.

Serves 8-10

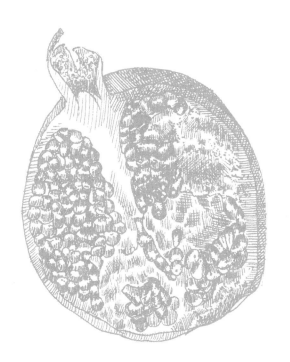

Eight

Juices & Drinks

Raw Family's Green Juice

This juice is yummy, full of nutrients, and can be made in a matter of minutes. Clean-up takes less than a minute!

Blend these ingredients well in a blender:

1	large bunch kale, chopped
2	medium apples, chopped
$1/2$	lemon with peel, chopped
1	cup water

Strain the liquid through a nut-milk bag or sprouting bag. **Serves 3-4**

Nut or Seed Milk

Any nut milk fits well for breakfast. It takes minutes to make. Nut milk is nutritious and light on the stomach

1	cup any nuts or seeds, soaked overnight
2	cups water
1	Tablespoon honey or 2-3 dates
1	teaspoon Celtic salt (optional)

Thoroughly blend all ingredients in a blender until smooth. Strain mixture through a sprout bag. Pour into a jar.   **Serves 4**

Sun Tea
This is a great drink on a hot summer day.
Sergei likes to drink sun tea after he runs. Sun tea is
a good substitute for black teas, green teas, and coffee.

1   bunch of each: peppermint, spearmint, lemon balm

Put in a gallon jar and fill with water. Let soak in sun for 8 hours or more until rich golden color.
                                    Yields 1 gallon

Un-Chocolate Almond Milk
This is a great liquid dessert.

1   quart almond milk
1/2   cup dates
1   young coconut (meat and water)
2   Tablespoons raw carob powder
1   raw vanilla bean

Blend well in a blender. Serve chilled.   **Serves 5-7**

Fancy Delicious Juice
Very unusual and tasty.

1   cantaloupe
1   pint fresh blueberries

Juice in a juicer and enjoy!   **Serves 2**

Joint Lubricator
This juice is good for making your joints more flexible.

1   bunch celery
2   cucumbers
1   apple to sweeten a little

Juice through a Champion Juicer, and drink fast before it oxidizes.   **Serves 1-2**

Ginger Snap Juice
This juice is nice chilled on a hot summer day.
It is a hit at parties.

8-10   apples
1   large piece ginger

Juice through Champion Juicer. Enjoy! **Serves 3-5**

Kale-idoscope
This juice is good chilled.

One bunch of your favorite kale
5   pears
1   lemon with peel

Juice through Champion Juicer.   **Serves 1-2**

Tomato Mania
This juice is nice to take to a potluck for yourself
when you are juice fasting! It's very filling.

8-10 large tomatoes
$^1/_2$ bunch celery
5-7   cloves garlic

Juice through the Champion Juicer.   **Serves 2-4**

Brook's Wine
This health juice tastes and looks like cabernet.

2   peeled beets
5-8   apples
1   lemon with peel

Juice through the Champion Juicer.   **Serves 1-2**

Crackers & Breads

Valya's Raw Bread

When this bread is finished, it looks like the real thing.

1	cup ground flax seeds
1	cup kamut, soaked overnight
1	cup walnuts, soaked overnight
1	cup chopped celery
2	teaspoons caraway seeds, soaked overnight
2	Tablespoons coriander
1	big onion
$^1/_2$	cup water
$^1/_2$	cup olive oil
$^1/_2$	cup raisins
	Juice of half a lemon
1	teaspoon salt

Blend soaked walnuts, kamut, and the onion in the food processor until finely chopped. Transfer to a bowl and mix with the ground flax seeds. Next, blend celery, olive oil, raisins, and water in a blender.

Combine both mixtures. Add the salt, coriander, lemon juice, and caraway, and mix thoroughly. Shape the mixture into small loaves and place on a Teflex dehydrator tray. Make sure to decorate your loaves with crushed nuts or poppy seed. Place in the dehydrator at 100 degrees, for about 24-36 hours. You may need to flip the bread after approximately 12-15 hours; this is so that both sides dry evenly. **Makes 5-7 loaves**

Igor's Crackers
These crackers make a good travel food.

Grind 2 cups of flaxseed in a dry Vitamix container.

Blend together:

1	cup water
1	large onion, chopped
3	stalks celery, chopped
4	cloves garlic, medium
2	tomatoes (optional)
1	teaspoon caraway seed
1	teaspoon coriander seed
1	teaspoon Celtic salt

Mix ground flaxseed into blended mix by hand. Dough should be slimy not dry. Cover the dough with cheesecloth or a towel and let sit in a bowl at a warm room temperature overnight to ferment slightly. If more sour taste is desired, ferment 2-3 days. Using a spatula spread on non-stick dehydrating sheets. Divide into squares of desired size. For softer bread, dehydrate

16 hours on one side, 4 hours on the other. For crispy crackers, dry well. Keep crackers refrigerated.

Yields 16 crackers.

Corn Chips
These chips actually turn out crunchy.

4	cups corn
1/4	cup olive oil
1/2	cup water
1/2	teaspoon salt
1/2	cup ground flax seeds (in coffee grinder or food processor)
2	chili peppers
1	Tablespoon honey
1	bunch cilantro

Blend all but flax; mixture will be somewhat thick. Add flax to thicken while blender is running. Spread on Teflex sheets. Turn and mark in triangles after a few hours. Dehydrate until crisp.

Simple Crackers
We like this recipe for its simplicity and taste.

2	cups whole flax seed
1	cup water
1/2	teaspoon salt

If you want to enhance the flavor, blend in a bunch of your favorite herbs and/or a tomato.

Mix and spread one-inch thick with a spatula on dehydrator sheets. Dehydrate for about 12 hours or until crisp.   **Yields 16 crackers**

Vrinda's So-Raw-Dough Crackers

If you miss sourdough bread, this recipe is for you.

3   cups almond pulp (from making milk)
1   cup golden flax seed
1   cup water
$1/2$ teaspoon caraway
$1/2$ teaspoon salt

Blend all ingredients in a food processor until smooth. Spread one-half-inch thick with a spatula on dehydrator sheets. Dehydrate for about 12 hours or until crisp.   **Yields 16 crackers**

Part Two
Desserts

L ive desserts are guilt free and good for you! In creating raw desserts, there is an unlimited variety of tastes, textures, and colors at hand. In our nine years of making raw gourmet food we have never made the same dessert twice. Use the following recipes as ideas to come up with your own raw desserts.

Ten

Smoothies

Sergei's Favorite Smoothie
According to Sergei,
"This is the easiest and best smoothie to make."

Blend the following ingredients in a blender until smooth:

2   oranges, peeled
2   frozen bananas (other frozen fruits are optional)

Place the oranges toward the bottom of blender to make enough liquid to blend the frozen bananas. Decorate with fresh strawberries!

Serves 2-3 (until you get addicted, then it serves only 1)

Deep Blue (with a little purple)

Blend the following ingredients in a blender until smooth:

2   frozen bananas
1   pint fresh ripe blueberries
1   cup orange juice

Serves 2-3

Duriano-Mania

Durian is an exotic spiky fruit from Thailand.

Blend the following ingredients in a blender until smooth:

$^1/_2$ cup durian meat

$^1/_2$ cup coconut meat (from young coconut)

2   cups coconut water

Serves 2-3

Banango Smoothie

You can make great parfait with this smoothie.

Blend the following ingredients in a blender until smooth:

2   frozen bananas

$1^1/_2$ cups frozen mango chunks
       (add more if desired)

1   cup orange juice

Cut up one fresh ripe mango into small cubes and mix into each cup for texture.   **Serves 2-3**

Nut Milk Shake

Wendy's does not even compete with this shake.

Blend the following ingredients in a blender until smooth:

3	cups almond milk
1/2	cup fresh or frozen strawberries
1	medium orange, peeled
1	fresh or frozen banana
2	Tablespoons honey or 1/4 cup pitted dates
1/2	teaspoon sea salt
1	vanilla bean
1/2	cup ice (ice is not necessary if you use frozen fruit)

Serves 6

Our First Smoothie

This smoothie turns out good every time.
It has impressed many people.

Blend the following ingredients in a blender until smooth:

2	frozen bananas
1/2	large avocado
1	pint strawberries
1	cup water

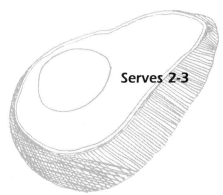

Serves 2-3

Chocolate Blizzard

This smoothie is excellent on a hot day.

Blend the following ingredients in a blender until smooth:

1	cup almond milk (Please see the recipe for almond milk in the drink section.)
2-3	frozen bananas (depending on how frozen you want it)
5-8	pitted dates
¹/₄	lemon with peel
3-5	Tablespoons raw carob (depending on how chocolatey you want it)
1	whole vanilla bean

Serves 2-3

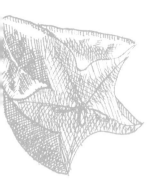

Cakes
& Pies

Directions on how to put a cake together:

Before putting a cake together, sprinkle a plate with something dry like ground nuts, carob powder, or shredded coconut so that the crust does not stick to the plate. Spread a layer of crust on to the plate. Next, make a layer of fruit, preferably fruit that isn't super juicy like oranges and pineapple. Things like bananas, blueberries, strawberries, raspberries, mangoes and young coconut work really well. Young coconut leaves a delicious looking white streak when the cake is cut. One or two types of fruit work best; any more than that makes it taste funny. Make another layer of crust on top of the fruit and then pour on the topping. Decoration is perhaps the most important thing in making a cake because when food is appealing to the eye, it's more enjoyable to eat. Use fresh fruits, berries and flowers for decoration. To make cakes look perfectly round and professional, you may use cheese cloth and a bowl of any shape or a spring form.

Generic Cake Recipe
We enjoy the flexibility of this recipe.
It has led us to many delicious creations.

Crust
Combine the following ingredients, mixing well:

1	cup ground nuts, seeds, or grains
1	Tablespoon oil
1	Tablespoon honey

Optional:

1/2	cup chopped or crushed fresh fruits or berries or 1/2 cup dry fruits, soaked for 1-2 hours, then ground
1	teaspoon vanilla
1/2	teaspoon nutmeg
1/2	cup raw carob powder
	Peel from 4 tangerines, well ground

If mixture is not firm enough, add psyllium husk, or shredded coconut. Form into crust on a flat plate.

Topping
Blend the following ingredients well; add water with a teaspoon if needed:

1/2	cup fresh or frozen fruit
1/2	cup nuts (white nuts look pretty)
1/2	cup olive oil
2-3	Tablespoons honey
	Juice of 1 medium lemon
1	teaspoon vanilla

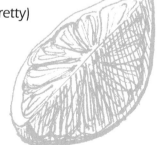

Spread evenly over the crust. Decorate with fruits, berries, and nuts. Give your cake a name. Chill.

Serves 8

Nuts, seeds and grains: almonds, walnuts, filberts, cashews, pine nuts, pecans, sunflower seeds, flaxseed, sesame or tahini, oat flour or rolled oats, buckwheat, kamut, barley.

Dried fruits: pitted prunes, raisins, apricots, dates, figs, currants.

Fresh fruits and berries: strawberries, apples, bananas, blueberries, pineapples, mangoes, apricots, raspberries, cranberries.

Almond Cake

This cake looks professional and is easy to cut.

Crust

3	cups ground almonds
1	Tablespoon oil
1/2	cup honey
1/2	teaspoon salt
1/2	cup chopped or crushed dates, soaked for 1-2 hours, then ground
1	teaspoon vanilla extract
1/2	cup raw carob powder
	Peel from 4 tangerines, well ground

If mixture is not firm enough, add psyllium husk, or shredded coconut. Form into crust on a flat plate.

Topping

Blend the following ingredients well; add water
with a teaspoon if needed:

    1/2   cup almonds
    1/2   cup olive oil
    2-3   Tablespoons honey
          Juice of 1 medium lemon
    1   teaspoon vanilla

Spread evenly over the crust. Decorate with fruits,
berries, and nuts. Chill.   **Serves 5**

Macadamia Date Pie

*Macadamia nuts and dates form a smooth yet solid crust.
Sometimes it's fun to make little sculptures out of it.*

Crust

    4   cups macadamia nuts
    2   cups dates
          Juice of one orange
    1   teaspoon salt
    1/2   teaspoon butterscotch or vanilla extract

Blend macadamia nuts in food processor until they
are finely chopped and transfer to a bowl. Blend the
dates and orange juice in a food processor and add to
the macadamia mix. Mix thoroughly together with salt
and butterscotch extract. Spread the crust out thinly

on a plate. Finely slice bananas or your favorite fruit and spread on top the macadamia date crust. Cover the fruit with another layer of the macadamia date mixture. Decorate the pie with thinly sliced oranges and nuts or your favorite fruits.

Serves 8

5-Minute Raw-Berry Shortcake
Of all of the cakes we make, this is one of the fastest and easiest to put together. It literally takes less than five minutes to make.

Crust
2	cups almonds
1/2	cup honey

Blend ingredients in a food processor until finely chopped.

Topping
1	cup walnuts
1/4	cup honey
2	Tablespoons fresh coconut butter (optional)

Blend ingredients in a blender until smooth. Richly decorate with fresh, sliced strawberries.

Serves 8

Sergei's Young Coconut Dream Cake

Sergei dreamed up this recipe on his 10th day of water fasting. This cake later won first place in a contest.

Crust

1	cup raw unsoaked walnuts
1/2	cup of your favorite pitted dates
1/2	cup young coconut water
4	Tablespoons raw carob

Blend the walnuts and dates in a food processor until the mixture is smooth. Mix in the carob and coconut water.

Icing

1	cup young coconut meat
1	Tablespoon honey
	Water, enough to blend into thick topping

Blend all the ingredients in Vitamix. Spread icing on cakes and decorate with fruit slices and nuts.

Serves 8

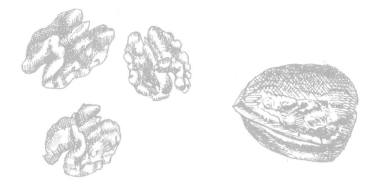

Cheesecake

3   cups pulp from making almond milk
2   cups strawberries or other berries
1/2 cup honey

Take the bowl of desired shape. Line it with cheese cloth. Put sliced strawberries on the bottom then put 1-inch layer of almond pulp. Put layer of sliced strawberries. Drizzle 1/2 of the honey over the strawberries. Put another layer of pulp. Put another layer of strawberries and honey. Continue until all ingredients have been used, making sure that the last layer is the pulp. Cover with a flat plate. Quickly, with both hands, rotate so plate is on the bottom. Gently tap on the bowl to loosen the cake. Gently remove bowl and cheese cloth.   **Serves 6**

Walnut Cream Cake
*The walnuts in both the crust and the topping
give this cake a unique unity in flavor, even
though the textures are different.*

Crust
Combine the following ingredients, mixing well:
1   cup ground walnuts
1   cup raisins
1   teaspoon vanilla

If mixture is not firm enough, add psyllium husk or shredded coconut. Form into crust on a flat plate.

Topping

Blend the following ingredients well; add water with a teaspoon if needed:

1/2	cup walnuts
2-3	Tablespoons raw honey
	Juice of 1 medium lemon

Spread evenly over the crust. Decorate with fruits, berries, and nuts. Chill. **Serves 12**

Wedding Cake

This cake does not need to be frozen because the crust is very firm. The more coconut you add, the firmer it will be. This wedding cake can easily sit out for several hours.

Crust

2	cups raw tahini
4	cups dry, shredded coconut
1/2	cup honey
1/2	teaspoon salt

Mix together until desired texture. For layers, use any sliced fruit of your choice.

Frosting

1	cup cashews
2	Tablespoons honey
1	teaspoon mint extract
1/4	cup fresh coconut butter
1/2	teaspoon salt
1/2	cup water

The cashews make the topping white. Try to use as little water as possible. The less water you use, the thicker it will be. Chill. You may buy the wedding cake stand at any craft store such as Michael's.

Serves 10-12

Pecan Pie

This pie is excellent for Thanksgiving and has a very pleasant, decadent taste.

Crust

2	cups ground pecans
2	cups figs
1	teaspoon nutmeg
2	teaspoon Nama Shoyu
	The peel of one lemon, well ground

Blend well in a food processor. For layers, use sliced strawberries or sliced banana.

Topping

1	cup walnuts or pecans
3	Tablespoons honey
1/2	teaspoon salt
1/2	cup water

Blend ingredients well and spread over crust. Decorate with pecans.

Serves 8

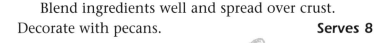

Un-Chocolate Cake

*The buckwheat soaks up the extra liquid
in the crust and becomes soft and crunchy.
The topping of this cake is out of this world!*

Crust

5	cups ground walnuts
3	cups raisins
3	Tablespoons raw carob powder
1	teaspoon Frontier's butterscotch flavor
1/2	teaspoon salt
1	cup dry, hulled buckwheat (optional)

Mix well. A nice thick layer of organic mango works great for the fruit layer.

Topping

1/2	cup water
1	cup raw tahini
4	Tablespoons honey
3	Tablespoons raw carob powder
1	teaspoon vanilla

It's important to put the water in first. The liquid makes it easier for the blender to work. Spread the topping evenly over the crust, or squeeze using decorating bag. Decorate with fruits, berries, and nuts. Chill.

Serves 12

Un-Chocolate Mousse Cake
This cake mostly resembles the cooked creamy cake.

Crust:

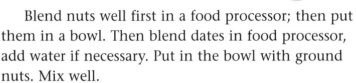

$1/2$ cup dates, pitted

$1/2$ cup walnuts

Blend nuts well first in a food processor; then put them in a bowl. Then blend dates in food processor, add water if necessary. Put in the bowl with ground nuts. Mix well.

In a spring form pan 6 or 7-inches wide:
Sprinkle $1/4$ cup of ground nuts on the bottom of spring form. Spread crust dough evenly on top of the layer of ground nuts. Slice 1 banana and layer over crust.

Brown Un-Chocolate Mousse:

2   cups dates, pitted

1   cup water

2   teaspoons vanilla

$1/2$ teaspoon sea salt

1   sliced lemon with peel

1   Tablespoon raw carob powder

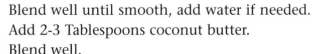

Blend well until smooth, add water if needed.
Add 2-3 Tablespoons coconut butter.
Blend well.

Serves 12

White Un-chocolate Mousse:

1	cups raw tahini
$^1/_2$	cup water
2	teaspoons vanilla
$^1/_2$	teaspoon sea salt
1	sliced lemon with peel

Blend well until smooth, add water if needed. Add 2-3 Tablespoons coconut butter. Blend well. Pour your mousse on top of layer of bananas. Chill in freezer for a couple of hours. Separate cake from the spring form with a knife before unlocking the spring form.

Serves 12-16

Twelve

Candies

Cream-Filled Delight

All children love these delicious treats,
and they especially like making them!

Crust

2	cups pecans
1/2	cup pitted dates
1	Tablespoon nutmeg
1/2	teaspoon salt

Blend in a food processor. Add a little bit of water or other liquid if the dates have a hard time blending.

Cream

1/2	cup pecans
1	Tablespoon raw carob
1	teaspoon vanilla extract or one vanilla bean
1/2	teaspoon salt
1/2	cup water

Blend in a blender until creamy. If you can get away with using less than 1/2 cup water and still being able to blend then go for it. Make small, 1-inch diameter balls. Press a thumbhole in the middle of the candy and fill with cream, then seal. Roll the candy in shredded coconut, crushed nuts, or poppy seeds. Chill for 2 hours in the freezer.   **Serves 6-12**

Sergei's Amazing Truffles

*We like to make some extra truffles, stash in
the freezer, and eat with our friends.*

1	cup unsoaked walnuts
1/2	cup of your favorite pitted dates
1/2	cup young coconut water
4	Tablespoons raw carob
1/2	teaspoon salt

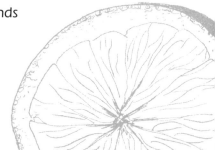

Blend the walnuts and dates in a food processor till the mixture is smooth. Mix in the raw carob and coconut water. Shape the mixture into small balls and roll the balls in carob. Decorate with your favorite fruit.   **Makes 8-12 truffles**

Cupcakes

*This recipe is useful in situations
such as parties and weddings when you're not
sure how many people will show up.*

5	cups unsoaked almonds
3	cups raisins
1/4	cup orange peel
1/4	cup orange juice

$^1/_2$ teaspoon salt
$^1/_2$ cup whole pine nuts

Use ice cream scoop to spoon mixture on to tray.

Crême Sauce

1   cup macadamia nuts
3   Tablespoons honey
$^1/_2$ teaspoon salt
$^1/_2$ cup water

Pour topping over cupcake and decorate with fruit of your choice.   **Serves 5-7**

Halvah

In a bowl mix:

16   ounces raw tahini
1   cup of shredded dried coconut
$^1/_2$ cup honey
$^1/_4$ teaspoon salt (optional)
$^1/_2$ cup pistachios (optional)

On a dehydrator tray, make a 2-inch thick cracker. Dry for 6-8 hours at 100 degrees F. Chill for 1-2 hours in a freezer before serving.   **Serves 24**

Thirteen

Cookies

A raw cookie is a mixture made with nuts, or seeds and chunks of fresh or dried fruit and then dehydrated. When making cookies, try to use a little bit of ingredients that will make them sticky such as dates, ground flax seeds, raisins, honey, etc. This will ensure that your cookie does not turn out too crumbly when finished. Cookies are an excellent traveling food.

Butternut Squash Cookies

These cookies are convenient for traveling.
They store well and are good to munch on in the car.

Ingredients:

4	cups peeled butternut squash, chopped into medium chunks
1	cup raisins
	Juice of one orange
1/2	teaspoon nutmeg
1	teaspoon cinnamon
3	Tablespoons raw honey

Blend the chopped squash in a food processor and transfer into a bowl. Next, blend the raisins and the orange juice in a food processor and add to the squash mixture. Add the rest of the ingredients into the bowl and mix thoroughly. Take out your ice cream scoop and scoop the mixture onto a dehydrator tray. Flatten each cookie until it is one inch thick. Set the dehydrator for 100 degrees and leave in 12–15 hours.

Makes 7-11 cookies

Alla's Cranberry Scones

These scones are an excellent holiday food.
They taste sweet and look very fancy.

Ingredients:

2	cups grated apples
2	cups carrot pulp after you make carrot juice
2	cups raisins or chopped dates
1	cup cranberries, fresh or dry
2	Tablespoons honey
2	cups almonds, ground
1	cup flaxseed blended with 1 cup water
1/4	cup olive oil

Mix well. You have to experiment to get the desired consistency. Shape into scones and put on dehydrator sheets. Dehydrate at 105-115 degrees for several hours; approximately 4 hours on one side, and then flip for 3 hours on opposite side.

Makes 24 scones

Valya's Almond Orange Cookies

Blend the following ingredients in a food processor until they are finely chopped:

4	cups raw almonds, soaked overnight
2	cups raisins
1/2	cup orange peel
2	medium oranges, whole
1/2	teaspoon salt
2	apples

When all the ingredients are finely processed, use a spatula to spread cookie mixture onto a dehydrator tray. Decorate each cookie with sliced nuts or raisins.

Makes 10-12 cookies

Te Bars

Our six-year-old friend, Tejas, created these delicious bars.

1 1/2	cup sprouted buckwheat groats
1/2	cup ground spelt
1/4	cup sunflower seeds, ground
1/3	cup olive oil
1/3	cup clover honey
1/2	cup carob
1/2	cup coconut, dried
1/2	teaspoon cinnamon
1/2	teaspoon vanilla
	Pinch of salt

Blend ingredients in a food processor. Dehydrate at 108 degrees, about 6 hours.   **Serves 8**

Macadamia Date Cookies

*These cookies are perfect for sneaking into theaters
with you. Not only do they look like regular cookies and fit
perfectly into your purse, but they also taste wonderful.*

4	cups macadamia nuts
2	cups dates
	Juice of one orange
1/2	teaspoon salt
1	teaspoon butterscotch or vanilla extract

Blend macadamia nuts in food processor until fine
and transfer to a bowl. Next, blend the dates and
orange juice in food processor and add to the
macadamia mix. Mix thoroughly together with salt
and butterscotch extract. Scoop the mixture out on to
Teflex dehydrator trays and decorate with pine nuts.
Set at 100 degrees and dehydrate for 12-15 hours.
Serve warm.

Makes 7-12 cookies

Sesame Cookies
*A fabulous way to use all the leftover
sesame pulp after making sesame milk.*

5   cups sesame seed pulp
2   cups raisins
3   Tablespoons raw honey
     Juice of one orange

Blend raisins and orange juice in food processor until mixture is finely puréed. Add to a bowl with the sesame seed pulp. Add honey and mix thoroughly. Spread the mixture onto Teflex dehydrator sheets, using a spatula, cut into squares. Sprinkle with poppy seeds and set in the dehydrator at 100 degrees. Dehydrate for 12-15 hours or until dry.

Makes 15-20 cookies

Fourteen

Pudding

Pudding is a good breakfast; it's fast, filling, and easy to make.

Chocolate Pudding

1	cup almond milk (see almond milk recipe on page 93
3	Tablespoons raw honey (or 10 pitted dates)
2	Tablespoons raw tahini
2	Tablespoons raw carob
$1/2$	teaspoon salt

Mix the ingredients in a blender until smooth. Add more tahini or carob if you like thicker pudding. Eat with strawberries. **Serves 5-7**

Psyllium Pudding

This dish is very elegant. We like to make it because people are impressed with how it looks and tastes.

Put clear cups on tray. Slice fruit of choice and put at bottom of cups.

Blend well:

2	cups water
1	teaspoon salt
1/2	cup honey or dates (remember that you're adding enough sweetness for the full blender)
2	Tablespoons vanilla extract
1	cup almonds
1/2	lemon with peel

The liquid will be thin. Add 8 to 9 teaspoons psyllium powder while blender is running. Quickly pour into cups over the fruit. You can make as many layers of psyllium and fruit as you like. The pudding will solidify in a matter of minutes.   **Serves 10-12**

Apple Sauce
One of our favorite breakfasts.

2	cups water
4	cups chopped apples
1	cup raisins
1/4	of a lemon with peel
1	teaspoon cinnamon

Begin to blend. While blending throw in more apples until desired thickness. Decorate with fresh berries or raisins.   **Serves 6**

Fifteen

Ice Cream

Ice cream is one of the most delicious and comforting foods. Nothing is better than ice cream for social events. Children and adults instantly like raw versions of ice cream. The greatest benefit of raw ice cream is that it closely resembles regular ice cream.

Vanilla Ice Cream

This ice cream will satisfy any ice cream lover.

4	cups water
3	Tablespoons honey or eight dates
2^1/$_2$	cup raw almonds
1	teaspoon salt

Blend in a blender until smooth and strain through a milk bag. Pour the milk into an ice cream maker and stir until firm (usually 12-20 minutes).

Note: You can make a sweet cheese out of the almond milk pulp.

Carob Delight

If you want to encourage kids in raw food, all
you have to do is serve them Carob Delight.

10	dates
4	cups water
4	Tablespoons raw carob powder
2¹/₂	cups almonds
1	teaspoon sea salt

Blend in a blender until smooth then strain through a milk bag. Pour into ice cream maker and stir until firm (usually 12-20 minutes).

Banana/Tahini Ice Cream

Sergei eats this ice cream year round, even when it snows.

4	frozen bananas
1	Tablespoon raw sesame tahini

Put ingredients through Champion Juicer with the blank on.

Optional ingredients:

Crushed nuts (sprinkled on top of ice cream)

1	teaspoon vanilla extract mixed into the ice cream

Serves 3

Berry Blitz

The berries give this ice cream different colors. It's fun to make colored layers of reds, blues, and purples.

4	frozen bananas
1	Tablespoon raw almond butter
1/2	cup frozen blue berries, blackberries, strawberries, etc.
1/2	cup fresh raspberries

Put all frozen ingredients through Champion Juicer with the blank on. Mix in 1/2 cup of raspberries and enjoy!   **Serves 3**

Jackfruit Ice Cream

If you are lucky enough to find jackfruit, this ice cream is worth living for!

1   cup frozen jackfruit pods (without the seeds)

Put through the Champion Juicer with blank on. Enjoy.   **Serves 1**

For those of you sitting there wondering what in the heck is jackfruit: The Jackfruit comes from the jackfruit tree, which is the largest tree in the world. It is native to Malaysia and India but grows throughout the tropics. Jackfruits are yellowish, greenish, or brownish and are usually the size of a medium melon. On the outside, the jackfruit is covered with dull little spikes. If you don't live anywhere tropical, don't fret, you still have a chance to acquire a jackfruit through an Asian or Thai market. By the way, the jackfruit tastes like the oh-so-famous chewing gum, Juicy Fruit. Or is it that Juicy Fruit tastes like jackfruit?!

Part Three
Travel foods

Travel foods are very important for staying on a raw food diet – whether you are traveling on an airplane, in a car, or backpacking. Raw travel foods are light, take up little space in your suitcase, and are easy to prepare. We have found there is lots of variety available, both sweet and savory.

Sixteen

Seasonings

Seasonings enhance the flavors that food already has. They instantly turn any bland dish into a delicious gourmet-tasting meal. When we travel, we always carry our own seasonings. They are light and easy to use. Seasonings have served us many times in airports, hotels, and restaurants.

Celery Salt Substitute
*Celery gives your salad a soft salty flavor
and is good for your digestion.*

20   pounds organic celery sticks

Dry for 24 hours in dehydrator until totally dry. Grind in Vitamix until fine powder.

Yields 1 quart of powder

Real Raw Healthy Sugar
*When we roll our candies in this it looks
just like powdered sugar.*

Peel and chop 20 pounds organic jicama. Dry for

24 hours or until totally dry in dehydrator. Grind in Vitamix until a fine powder, then put through pepper mill or coffee grinder to make finer, or run longer in the Vitamix.

Yields 1 quart of powder

Quickie Dressing
During the first two years on raw food, we were carrying this dressing with us everywhere, and we always kept a bottle of it in the car. Quickie helped us to enjoy meals in unknown restaurants, to participate in unexpected parties, and to create tasty salads "from scratch."

1/3   cups oil
1/3   cup apple cider vinegar
1/3   cup Nama Shoyu

Pour into bottle and shake.   **Serves 4**

We like a variety of shakers with dry seasonings on our table. Here are some of our favorite ones:

Gomasio
1/2   cup ground coriander
1/2   cup ground sesame seeds
1/2   cup ground flax seeds

Yields 1 1/2 cups

Thai Blend

¹/₂   cup ground dry ginger

¹/₂   cup ground parsley flakes

¹/₂   cup ground coriander

Yields 1¹/₂ cups

Sea Blend

¹/₂   cup granulated nori

¹/₂   cup granulated dulse

¹/₂   cup ground flax seeds

Yields 1¹/₂ cups

Spicy Blend

¹/₂   cup ground dry ginger

¹/₂   cup ground dry dill weed

¹/₂   cup ground flax seeds

Yields 1¹/₂ cups

Salty & Spicy Blend

¹/₂   cup granulated garlic

¹/₂   cup ground dry dill weed

¹/₂   cup ground dry celery

Yields 1¹/₂ cups

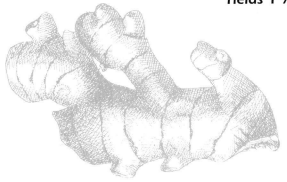

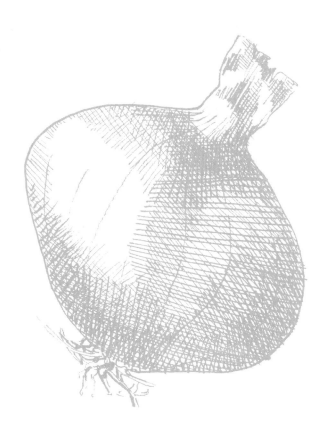

Seventeen

Quick Mixes

Quick Mix Soup
This is an excellent airplane food!

Slice or chop these ingredients:

15	white mushrooms
5	carrots, grated
4	white onions
3	colored bell peppers
3	tomatoes
1	bunch celery
1	bunch parsley

Dry all ingredients in a dehydrator for 18-24 hours or until dry. When dry, mix all of them together. To prepare soup, put 1/4 cup of dry veggies into 1 cup of warm (not hot) water with a 1 Tablespoon of oil and salt to taste. Let it sit and soak in the juices for 10-15 minutes and enjoy!   **Serves 8-10**

Buckwheat Millet Morning Cereal

This cereal is tasty and convenient for traveling.

Soak the following overnight:

1	cup millet
2	cups buckwheat
1	cup coarsely chopped hazel nuts

Additional ingredients:

1	cup raisins
3	Tablespoons honey
1	teaspoon cinnamon

Using a rolling pin, flatten the millet and the buckwheat. Transfer the grains into a bowl and add the crushed hazel nuts. Next, add the rest of the ingredients and mix thoroughly. Spread the mixture out evenly onto a dehydrator sheet. Avoid spreading the mixture too thick. Set the dehydrator for 105 degrees and wait until the cereal is completely dry, which will take between 10–12 hours. Serve with nut milks.

Makes 6 servings

Eighteen

Trail Mixes

These make a good snack. They are filling but will not make you feel heavy, and best of all, they are easy to pack.

Better Than Roasted Sunflower Seeds
These sunflower seeds turn out light and crispy.

9   cups raw sunflower seeds soaked for 8 hours and dried for 4 hours

2   cups Nama Shoyu (or 3 Tablespoons sea salt)
    Enough water to submerge the seeds an inch

2   Tablespoons turmeric powder

2   Tablespoons raw honey (optional)

1   teaspoon cayenne powder

Mix all ingredients well in a gallon jar. Let the seeds soak for 12 hours. Spread out onto Teflex sheet and dry in dehydrator for 18-24 hours or until totally crunchy and crisp.

Note: if you are using Nama Shoyu or another raw soy sauce, then you know how expensive it is. After the seeds are done soaking, drain the fluid into a container and use it in a

salad or to season a dressing, or simply as a salt substitute.)
These make a really good snack; they are filling but will not make you feel heavy and best of all, they are easy to pack.

**Yields approximately 1 pound
of ready-to-eat mix**

Sweet Crunchy Walnuts

*This recipe is a good substitute for
popcorn in movie theaters.*

9	cups walnuts, un-soaked
2	cups Nama Shoyu or 3 Tablespoons salt
	Enough water to submerge the walnuts an inch
3	Tablespoons Hungarian paprika
3	Tablespoons raw honey
1	teaspoon cayenne powder

Mix all ingredients in a gallon jar. Let the seeds soak for 24 hours. Spread out onto Teflex sheet and dry in dehydrator for 18-24 hours or until totally crunchy and crisp.

Note: if you are using Nama Shoyu or another raw soy sauce then you know how expensive it is. After the seeds are done soaking drain the fluid into a container and use it in a salad or to season a dressing, or simply as a salt substitute.

**Yields approximately 1 pound
of ready-to-eat mix**

Amazing Almonds

We like to take these almonds on hikes with us because they are so yummy and filling.

9   cups almonds soaked 8 hours and
     dried 4 hours
2   cups Nama Shoyu or 3 Tablespoons salt
     Enough water to submerge the almonds
     an inch
2   Tablespoons garlic powder
2   Tablespoons raw honey (optional)
1   teaspoon cayenne powder

Mix all ingredients in a gallon jar. Let the seeds soak for 12 hours. Spread out onto Teflex sheet and dry in dehydrator for 18-24 hours or until totally crunchy and crisp.

Note: if you are using Nama Shoyu or another raw soy sauce then you know how expensive it is. After the seeds are done soaking drain the fluid into a container and use it in a salad or to season a dressing, or simply as a salt substitute.

**Yields approximately 1 pound
of ready-to-eat mix**

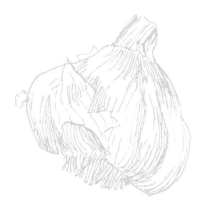